...nie pended, I
you. holde true
Love
Penny

ANY ROUGH
TIMES ARE NOW
BEHIND YOU

ANY ROUGH TIMES ARE NOW BEHIND YOU

SELECTED POEMS AND WRITINGS: 1979–1995

DAVE ALVIN

INCOMMUNICADO PRESS
P.O.BOX 99090, SAN DIEGO CA 92169 USA

©1995, 1996 INCOMMUNICADO
Contents ©1986, 1995 Dave Alvin

ISBN # 0-884615-09-0
Second printing.

Cover and book design by Gary Hustwit.
Front cover photo of motel by Jeudi Tabler. Photo of Dave and
Wolf by Cass Alvin. Back cover photo by Beth Herzhaft.
Bio page photo by Steve Smith.
Edited by Gary Hustwit.

THANKS: Nicole Panter (for friendship and editing), Richard Lee,
Elliot Fried, Cass and Nana Alvin, Gary Hustwit, Laura Cloud,
Susan Rome, Jill Jordan, Lisa Mednick, Iris Berry, Rosemarie
Patronette, Exene Cervenka, Harvey Kubernick, Michael C. Ford
and everyone else.

Some of the material included has previously appeared in the
following magazines: *Caffeine, The A.K.A.Review, Rattler,
Asymptote* and *Enclitic,* as well as the anthologies *Nude Erections,
Hit and Run Poets* and *Poetry Loves Poetry—An Anthology of Los
Angeles Poets.* Some selections originally appeared on the spoken
word albums *Voices of the Angels, English As a Second Language,
Neighborhood Rhythms* and *Side Effects.* Also included are poems
from Dave Alvin's *Nana, Big Joe and the Fourth of July* (Illiterati).

Printed in the U.S.A.

CONTENTS

For Gerald Locklin, Lee Allen, Mary Zerkie and Wolf.

ANY ROUGH TIMES ARE NOW BEHIND YOU

PAULINE, ROCKET SHIPS AND
THE ORANGE GROVE MANSION

In 1960
everything in my hometown was new.
New streets with new curbs
in front of new tract homes.
New, skinny trees
grew from new lawns.
New pavement
surrounded new supermarkets
where new mothers
parked their new cars.
New children walked home
on new sidewalks
from new schools.
In 1960
everything in my hometown was new
except the orange groves.

An orange grove
had been bulldozed
to build a new bank.
To celebrate the bank's grand opening
the bank gave every kid,
who started a five dollar savings account,
a rocket ship piggy bank.
Rocket ships were important
in my hometown in 1960.
A mile from the new bank,

North American Rockwell
had bulldozed
hundreds of acres of orange groves
to build their design and construction facilities
where real rocket ships were made.

My mother's best friend, Pauline,
took my brother and I
to the grand opening of the bank.
Our mother gave us five dollars each
and Pauline gave us nickels
to put in our rocket ship banks.

Pauline had come to California
from Oklahoma during the 1930s.
My brother and I were too young
to know about the dust bowl migration
or even Oklahoma.
Downey, California was the whole world
and the whole world was new.

Pauline had a thick accent
and we made fun of it
behind her back.
She wore old dresses,
drove an old car
and already had a grown son
named Billy Bob.
When she'd tell me stories
about her childhood in Oklahoma,
I'd hum songs to myself
or stare at my fingernails.

When she tried to hug me,
which was often,
I'd hide in the bathroom
and lock the door.
Pauline would stand outside the door
and shout in her Oklahoma accent,

DAVID ALBERT ALVIN!
YOU GIT OUT HERE RIGHT NOW!
I JUST WANT TO GIVE YOU A BIG LOVE HUG.

I'd sit on the toilet seat
chanting under my breath,

GO AWAY, GO AWAY, JUST GO AWAY.

Whenever she would trap me
and hold me on her lap,
she'd softly sing old songs.
Sometimes I'd fall asleep as she sang
but just as often
I'd stare at her grey hair
and her wrinkled skin.
I'd smell her sweat and perfume,
trapped in her fat but strong arms,
smothered by her oldness.

From the new bank,
Pauline drove my brother and I
down Florence avenue
past groves of grey, dying orange trees
waiting for bulldozers.

Eventually she turned onto a dirt road
and drove through one of the groves
until we reached a deserted two story,
Spanish-style mansion.
Pauline stopped the car
and we got out and joined a small crowd
watching as a wrecking ball
pounded chunks out of the mansion's stucco walls.
I saw a dead orange tree
thrown into a drained swimming pool.

I JUST WANTED TO SEE THIS, HONEY.
I remember Pauline saying.

Years later,
when I knew about the dust bowl and Okies
and Woody Guthrie and John Steinbeck
and Merle Haggard,
I wondered why Pauline
wanted to see the old mansion torn down.

Maybe she always dreamed
of living in that mansion.
Maybe she once knew the people
who lived in it.
Maybe, back in the '30s,
she and her family worked in the groves
surrounding the mansion,
picking oranges for two and a half cents a box
while the mansion's owners
swam in the pool
and drank orange juice
in the cool shade of the arched stucco patio.

Maybe the owner's son
made love to her one night
in a dark orange grove.
Maybe he left her heartbroken
in the soft, cold dirt
beneath the trees.

Or maybe Pauline
just liked seeing buildings torn down.

I JUST WANTED TO SEE THIS, HONEY.

Pauline might have said more.
She might have explained everything
but I don't remember
because I'd stopped listening.

I was too busy
holding my new rocket ship
in front of my squinted eyes
and making the sounds of exploding bombs.
I imagined that the bombs
from my rocket ship
were knocking down the walls
of the old mansion
and leveling
the grey, dying orange trees.

BOYS WITHOUT DATES

1

Tony and Victor Santiago shared
a beat up, '50s Nash Rambler.

For fun, Tony and Victor would
call the cops and report
seeing a couple of teenage boys
putting a dead body into the trunk
of a '50s Nash Rambler
then they'd drive around
Bellflower, Lakewood and Downey
hoping to get pulled over.

On weekend nights, Tony and Victor
liked to drive the Rambler
across the lawns of tract homes
and steal the plaster animals
decorating the front yards.

After a couple of weeks
they'd return the stolen lawn animals
with typewritten notes
from the plaster animals to their owners
describing all the fun they had on vacation
but how happy they were
to finally be back home.

When Tony started dating a girl named Peggy,
Victor started drinking alone.

He listened to atonal, avant garde jazz
and read old books from the sixties
that he'd stolen from a used book store
(books that predicted the coming
revolution that never came).

Believing he was keeping the fires of '60s revolt
from burning out in the mid-'70s,
Victor would drive alone in the Rambler
late at night through rich neighborhoods,
smashing the windows of Cadillacs and Porsches,
wondering why no one he went to school with
wanted to build bombs.

2

When Daniel was fifteen
his best friend, Gary,
was twenty-one
and lived in the bathroom
of a laundromat.

They'd smoke pot in Daniel's bedroom
in the afternoon when Daniel would
come home from school
and they'd only listen
to old fifties doo-wop records
even though it was 1972.

Gary would tell Daniel stories
about running away from home for good
when he was thirteen,
about what an asshole his father had been,
about how he lived in Compton for a while
with a couple members of the R+B vocal group
The Olympics,
about how nobody makes good records
like the oldies anymore,
about dropping acid and hitchhiking
to the Monterey Pop festival in '67,
about how he didn't dig the music
but he dug the drugs,
about living on the streets in San Francisco,
about coming back to Downey
because his mother got him a job
as a janitor at a junior high school,
about how he lost the job after a week
because he got caught buying
a joint off one of the students
and about how the bathroom
at the laundromat was carpeted
so it wasn't such a bad place to crash.

In the evenings
Daniel would make
white bread and American cheese sandwiches
and they'd eat them walking to the laundromat.

When they'd say goodbye,
Gary would always thank Daniel
for the sandwiches and tell him
that he was cool.

Walking home alone,
Daniel did feel cool
because a cool, older guy
had told him he was cool
and he knew it was just a matter of time
before all the girls knew it too.

3

Rory Thomas worked every morning
at his parents' dairy farm in Artesia
and came to school smelling of cowshit.

He smoked filterless Camels,
wore straight leg Levis instead of bell bottoms
and his favorite singer was Buck Owens
instead of Cat Stevens, who all the girls loved.

Rory's only friends in high school
were two boys who also worked at local dairies
and also smelled of cowshit.

One Saturday night, when he was a junior,
Rory got drunk on Boone's Farm Apple Wine,
snuck onto the high school campus,
and kicked down the low brick wall
that surrounded senior square,
brick by brick,
with the heels of his black cowboy boots.

The following Monday, angry seniors
blamed the Paramount High football team,
the South Gate High football team
or some anti-social stoners.

From then on,
Rory and his two friends
called his cowboy boots
"the great equalizers."

4

Jimmy's father fell asleep, drunk,
at the kitchen table
still wearing his bloody butcher's apron.

Jimmy's mother stretched out on the couch
in front of the tv, wearing fuzzy, high heel slippers
and smoking Lucky Strikes.

Jimmy's brother, just home from Vietnam,
laid in his bed listening to Jethro Tull on headphones,
nodding out on heroin.

Jimmy smoked a joint
in his bedroom closet,
burning incense and a candle,
staring at the posters of rock stars
that covered the closet walls,
listening to his father snore,

listening to his mother coughing
as she changed channels with the remote control,
listening to his brother's foot gently tapping
against his bedroom wall.

A TRIP WITH HER FATHER

Her father rode in the backseat
as I drove her up Highway 101
late one night.
My hand between her legs,
hers between mine.
We listened to R+B oldies
while she and I,
kissing whenever the road was clear,
swapped obscene true stories from our lives.

When we stopped for the night,
we put her father on a table in the motel room
as she and I fucked
with the television and all the lights on.
The next morning we left him in the car
as we ate breakfast in San Luis Obispo.

Later that day,
when we hiked down to a deserted beach
near Big Sur,
she gathered wildflowers in her straw hat
while I carried her father.
She'd brought her father with her from Baltimore
when she'd moved to California five years earlier.
She had taken him
from apartment to apartment
and from lover to lover until she met me.

When we reached the beach
she took her father from me
and set the coffee can down on the sand.
She turned her back for only a moment
to grab the flowers from her hat
when a large wave knocked the can over
and carried the contents out to sea.

She cried as I held her,
upset that she didn't have a chance
to say a more formal goodbye.

FOURTH OF JULY IN THE DARK

After work I'd go to her apartment.
Sometimes she'd have dinner ready
and everything would be fine.
Sometimes, though, she'd have all the lights off.
She would lay face down
on the living room floor,
her arms covering her eyes.
In the dark.
No T.V.
No radio.
No records.
Silence.
In the dark.

Some nights I'd lie next to her
not talking,
digging my face into the carpet with her.
Some nights we'd fight,
neither of us taking our faces from the carpet.
Some nights I'd sit on the top of the stairs
outside the apartment, smoking cigarettes
because she didn't allow smoking inside.
On those nights
I'd eat Pup 'n' Taco for dinner on the stairs
and stare at the neighborhood.

It was a dead end street
of run-down, early-sixties apartments

and two-story duplexes
with only three sickly palm trees on the block.
People parked their cars on what little lawns they had.
Everything in the neighborhood
was coated with yellow shadows
from the orange security lights of the Coca-Cola
bottling plant around the corner.
The white kids sat around their vans, drinking beer,
listening to FM rock.
The Mexican kids sat on their porches, drinking beer,
listening to AM oldies.
And she lay with her face to the floor
in the dark.

Two years before
she lived in Northern California, in the forest,
going to college, making ceramics,
eating natural foods and writing poetry
but something drug her down here.
Drug her down here
to a factory day job in Northwest Long Beach.
Drug her down here
to a family who made her stay
in the apartment they still owned
but in a neighborhood they'd abandoned.
Drug her down to a chain smoking boyfriend happy
to make minimum wage as a bad cook.

Something drug her down to the floor.

On the fourth of July,
The Mexican kids shot off fireworks in the street.

The white kids watched from the other side of the street.
I watched from the top of the stairs, smoking
as she laid on the floor
in the dark.

THE CROW'S POLKA

He was drunk, drunk, drunk
that afternoon.

Not drunk,
the way he'd get on Saturday nights
when he'd play his polka records
full blast on the stereo
and dance in the living room
in only his t-shirt and boxers,
singing along in Polish.

Not drunk, drunk
the way he'd get when company was over
and he wanted everyone to know
that he'd been everywhere
and done everything
and everyone
and everything
was full of shit.

No,
he was drunk, drunk, drunk
that afternoon
and the front yard was full of crows
and he hated crows.

So he got his German shotgun
and blew one of the crows to bits.

Neighbors came out of their houses
and he flipped them off
because he was drunk, drunk, drunk.
and they were all full of shit anyway.

One of them said that it wasn't a crow he shot
but a dove.

BULLSHIT he said.

He went back into the house
and sat at the kitchen table
with his half-empty, half-gallon bottle of vodka
and the shotgun resting in his lap.

Then he got drunk, drunk, drunk, drunk,
and passed out
as the crows returned
to the front yard.

MY BROTHER

1

Somewhere in the southwest,
in some diner, my brother
was six or seven
and I was maybe four,
maybe five.

I knew he was my brother
but I think it was the first time
I ever recognized him
by his face as my brother.

We were traveling with our father
on one of his union organizing field trips
and my brother
held a plastic toy airplane
in front of me that he'd taken
from a rack of toys.

He smiled
and pointed to the toy plane
and then to me
and then to our father
sitting at a table across the diner.

He walked over to our father,
smiling, pointing to the toy

and then to me
but our father just yelled at him.

My brother and I were crying,
and our father was still yelling,
as my brother put the toy plane
back onto the rack of toys
he'd taken it from.

2

I went down quick.

One punch to my stomach,
three to my head
from the guy with black hair.

The other two guys had my brother
on the other side of our car.

He stood straight and proud,
with his hands in fists
at his sides.

DO YOU REALLY WANT TO FIGHT?
he said as they took turns
hitting him in the face.

Both got angrier with each punch
because my brother,

his face red but not bloody,
refused to fight back.

IF YOU REALLY WANT TO FIGHT,
I'LL KILL YOU.
he repeated calmly
as he took every punch.

It might have been our hair,
greased and pompadoured
before that was back in style,
or maybe our leather jackets
or maybe the three marines
were just drunk and pissed
they hadn't gotten laid in Hollywood
or maybe they were just drunk
and wanted to see blood.

The blonde one, wearing a t-shirt
of the marines raising the flag on Iwo Jima,
started the fight
as my brother and I
were getting some Pioneer Chicken to go.

It was after two in the morning
and we were on our way home
from some party.

The other two marines joined in
as the chicken employees
watched expressionless,
doing nothing.

I pulled myself up against our car
and watched as the black haired marine
joined the other two punching
my brother.

IF YOU REALLY WANT TO FIGHT
I'LL KILL YOU.
my brother repeated
as black hair's punches
did no more damage
than his friends' punches had.

When black hair tired,
Iwo Jima took over again.

Then I heard it clearly.

The sharp cracks
of breaking bones.

I FUCKING BROKE MY WRIST
Iwo Jima screamed
HIS FUCKING FACE IS LIKE
FUCKING CONCRETE.

Then they left
cursing my brother
and his hard head.

THE THING TO REMEMBER
my brother said
as we drove home to Downey,
IS THAT IT DOESN'T HURT

WHEN THEY HIT YOU,
IT ONLY HURTS LATER.

When we got home,
I washed the blood off my face,
then my brother and I
ate the cold chicken
and fell asleep
watching television.

LAKE ELSINORE

Lake Elsinore is not the prettiest lake.
Trailer parks in the middle of treeless,
dusty fields, condominiums that got lost
on their way to Orange County in the middle of
dusty, treeless fields.

Industrial parks that look like waffle griddles,
painted with absurd stripes of pink and yellow,
sitting in dusty fields next to dusty palm trees
next to a new four lane highway whose blacktop
is so hot it just throws the heat back at
the sun, like a dare.

Much of the outskirts is taken up with what
real estate men call "ranches." Some are well
made houses sitting on five acres but most
are mobile homes stuck on one acre of dead grass.
Most have only potted plants, hanging from their
metal porches for shade.

You can smell the non-stop air conditioning inside.
You can feel the dirty heat beating the tin roofs.
You can guess the owners' life stories.
You can guess how many times they've been married.
You can imagine their air conditioned, tin roof sex life.
You can imagine the rock star posters on the kids' walls.
You can guess what the kids dream about.
You can guess if their parents still do.

And if you're very quiet,
late in the afternoon,
one of these mobile home ranchers will come outside
and water his dry grass
and if you're very, very quiet
you can hear the hot wind chafe his lips.

1969

We hiked in the Sierra for two weeks.
Three men: Jack, Tex and my father.
Three boys: my brother Phil,
his friend Doug and me.
My father carried most of the weight,
ninety pounds
of cooking utensils, tube tents,
a sleeping bag along with a few
carefully wrapped bottles of vodka.

The first night that we camped along the Kern River,
a bear or racoons got into our food box
and ate all our meat,
leaving us with only dehydrated fruits
and powdered soup.

In the evening
the men would sit at the campfire
farting and smoking,
passing one of the vodka bottles
and passing old stories.
Tex had several different stories
of how he lost his thumb.
Jack had the Korean War
and being a teenage bellboy
in a downtown Fresno hotel-whorehouse
and bloody murder scenes he covered
as a L.A.P.D. artist.

My dad had World War Two
and riding the Depression rails
and union organizing in the southwest.
Stories of cowboys on warm nights,
fights in dark bars,
poor G.I.s that met the wrong hookers,
G.I.s that liked other G.I.s
drinking binges in liberated Paris
and the more noteworthy sights of the world.

FUCK THE ALPS! My father would say.
I'VE SEEN 'EM AND THEY DON'T TOUCH THESE SIERRAS.

WELL, I'VE SEEN SOME PARTS OF ITALY
THAT ARE PRETTY NICE, CASS. Jack would answer.

OH, FUCK YOU, JACK.

Every night Doug would creep into the woods
and not return
until the men had exhausted
their life stories
and gone to bed.

THAT BOY IS AN ODD ONE
Tex would say
as Doug slipped into the dark trees.
WHAT DO YOU THINK HE DOES OUT THERE, JACK?
JERK OFF OR SOMETHING?

My father would mime jacking off
with an exaggerated grin.
HE'S JUST AN ASSHOLE. WHO CARES.

Phil would read books by flashlight
and sneak a cigarette or two in his tent.
I would try to sleep in my bag,
listening to the men talk,
praying the mountain trip would end
so I could go home to hamburgers
and rock and roll records.
We lost the main trail for two days
and Jack invented a path across several ridges
of dry manzanita to Rattlesnake Creek.
From there it would be an easy hike
back to Kern River.
The manzanita ripped through our shirts
and tore at our skin.
My father fell twenty feet or so
down a cliff of loose dirt
but broke none of the precious vodka bottles.

We camped in a small clearing
on the banks of Rattlesnake Creek.
I played with a crawfish.
I let him crawl up and down my arm.

AIN'T NO CRAWFISH IN CALIFORNIA, FUCKHEAD
THAT'S A SCORPION. Phil laughed.

I hurled the scorpion into the creek
and said fuck for the first time in front
of my father.

That night Jack
told us about the murder scenes he had covered:

the positions of the bodies,
how they had been mutilated,
how they had died,
fast or slow.
My father talked about when his Signal Corps
unit had liberated a concentration camp.
He had to photograph the survivors.
He had to photograph the dead in mass graves.
He had to photograph their teeth
for possible identification.
Tex tried to talk about knife sharpening
or the next day's fishing
or Oklahoma hookers
but the other two men drank
and told their stories without laughing.

In the daytime, as we hiked,
Doug and Phil lectured me in growing up.
They were high school juniors
and in September I was going to be a freshman.
They told me how to pick up high school girls
and what to do if I got one.
They told me what to drink
and where to drink it,
what to smoke and where to smoke it.
Near the end of the trip
I got up the nerve to ask Doug
what he did alone in the
woods after dark.

I JUST WRITE IN MY NOTEBOOK. he said.

WRITE WHAT?

STUFF YOU WOULDN'T UNDERSTAND.

Phil took me aside.
He said that even he didn't know
what Doug was doing but he was pretty sure
that Doug was taking LSD.
I didn't know what that meant then
but it sounded important.

After ten days of sun and heat
the weather turned to rain and hail
for four days running.

The creeks and rivers were flowing mud.
We strained the dirty water
through shirts and rags
and then boiled it before drinking.
There was no hope of fishing.
The men ran out of stories
and the evenings were spent
cursing the weather
and cursing the boys.

I NEVER SHOULD HAVE LISTENED TO YOU, CASS.
BRINGING FUCKING KIDS LIKE THESE UP HERE.
I'VE HAD SCOUT TROOPS OF GODDAMN EIGHT
YEAR OLDS MORE MATURE.
Jack said, sure that we heard him.

I WONDER ABOUT THE FUTURE OF OUR
COUNTRY SOMETIMES. Tex whispered.

YOU'RE ALL GRANDMOTHERS. My father ended it.

It was over.
The fishing had been bad,
the weather either too hot or too cold,
the trails lost.

After a two-day hike,
we made our way to Cottonwood Creek
where there was a telephone.
My father called my mother
and she drove up from Los Angeles
to pick us up.

In Lone Pine
we ate our first meat in two weeks
in an all-night diner.
Tex came into the diner
and threw a newspaper on the table.

LOOKS LIKE YOU'LL BE BUSY WHEN YOU GET
HOME, JACK.

Jack shook his head.
HERE IT GOES AGAIN.
On the front page was a photo of Sharon Tate.
The old men had never heard of her.

HOLLYWOOD MASS MURDER, the headline said.

My father looked out the window
at the Sierra rising from the Owens Valley
in the moonlight.

Then he turned to me and smiled,
WELL, PEOPLE ARE FUCKED.

I went to the bathroom.
In the mirror I saw
one black hair on my chest.

DRUNK 1985
for Joe and Jimmy Liggins

He woke up with a blonde
next to him in bed.

He couldn't remember her name.

He looked around the room
and saw his boots and her boots
thrown on the floor
and he saw the black leather pants
and jacket
she had been wearing the night before
tangled up with his Levis.

Then he remembered being in some bar
and the blonde in black leather
talking to him as he bought the drinks.

He remembered her telling him
about just getting back to California
after stripping for two months in Hawaii.

She said something about her husband,
something about what an asshole he was.

He remembered saying something
about how a beautiful woman like her
shouldn't be married to some asshole.

She said something about all men
were assholes
and he remembered saying something like,
all men weren't assholes,
baby.

Then she said prove it.

When the blonde in bed next to him woke up,
they had sex.

She told him she loved him
as he tried to remember her name.

She told him she loved him
because he was so brave and honest.

She told him no one else would have done
what he had done
as he tried to remember exactly
what it was he had done.

He remembered the blonde hair,
the black leather pants and the drinks
as she told him that she was now his
but he didn't remember much else
until she was on top of him
and the bedroom door opened.

A little girl,
four or five years old walked in
and stood at the edge of the bed

watching them have sex,
and said,
MOMMY, IS THIS WHERE WE LIVE NOW?

Then he remembered going to an apartment
on a side street in east Hollywood
and peeking through a door left half open
as the blonde in black leather kissed some guy
who was sitting in a chair watching television.

Then he remembered sneaking into the apartment
as the blonde went down on the man in the chair.

Then he remembered going into a bedroom,
and taking a little girl out of her bed.

Then he remembered the little girl asking him,
as he carried her out to his car,
ARE WE GOING SOMEPLACE NICE?

Then he remembered telling her,
YES, WE'RE GOING SOMEPLACE NICE.

A POEM FOR DEMI MOORE'S MOTHER

This afternoon,
at a truck stop outside Amarillo,
I saw nude photos of you
in some porno magazine
recreating famous scenes
from your daughter's movies.

Your alcoholic eyes, staring desperately
from the magazine's pages,
reminded me of a just-kicked dog
that doesn't understand why it was just kicked.

Now, it's after midnight
and I'm driving west on Interstate 40
past an exit sign for Las Vegas, New Mexico,
where the porno magazine said you lived.

Looking through the window of my van
at the stars above the dark, empty highway,
I imagine you leaving some bar, drunk,
and glancing at the same stars
so far away.

Those stars are so far away,
farther away than Santa Fe's millionaire adobes
or the private beaches of Malibu.

They're too far away
to hear your barroom flirtations
or the old songs fading in and out on my radio.

Too far to care if you leave the bar with a stranger
and too far to smell his warm beer breath
on your neck.

Too far to care if I drive
off the road into a ditch
or if I smoke myself to death.

Those stars are too far away
to see how old your face looks
when his lips and your sweat
rub away your make-up
and too far away to see how old mine looks
in the rear view mirror.

Maybe their distant,
indifferent beauty exists
not to guide us,
like signs along the interstate,
but only to measure
how far we have fallen.

I throw a burning cigarette
out of the van window
and watch the butt explode
on the black pavement,
in the black night,
like a newborn galaxy.

SAN FERNANDO VALLEY NO. 1

I was in a bar
in the north San Fernando Valley
drinking beer with an old friend.
He had just moved back
to his mother's tract home in the valley
from New York's lower east side.
He did most of the talking.
The pressure of being
a minor rock cult hero
had given him a drug problem
and a breakdown.
Or so he said.
    This fucking manager.
    That fucking record company.
    This fucking guitar player.
    That fucking agent.
    This fucking girlfriend.
    That fucking critic.
He was doing better now, he said,
but it was going to take time to completely recover.
Some middle-aged man sat two stools down
drinking whiskey.
As my friend talked, the older man
put Merle Haggard's GOIN' WHERE THE LONELY GO
on the jukebox.
As he sat back down
the middle-aged man softly placed
his hands around his drink

and mouthed the song lyrics along with Merle.
I could see that his hands were bloody
and wrapped with torn rags.
Now, barroom etiquette says
you never bother a man drinking alone
who's singing along with a sad song,
especially one with bloody hands.
So I didn't.
My friend didn't see the older man.

He went on about another fucking manager.
        And another fucking record company.
        And another fucking guitar player.
        And another fucking girlfriend.
        And another fucking critic.
It's been tough, my friend said,
as the older man rubbed
the bloody hands and rags together,
but it should be better in time.

EAST HOLLYWOOD

The opossum,
like the three Nicaraguans
who captured it with a clothes hanger
fashioned into a noose,
is not native
to California.

Neither
is the drunk English woman
screaming at the Nicaraguans
to let the opossum loose.

The opossum,
one of the men tries to explain
in broken english,
had bitten a kid.

The opossum,
the woman tries to explain
in slurred english,
is innocent and helpless.

The opossum
slaps its tail wildly in the air,
gasping for breath,
as they argue.

THE HEAVYWEIGHT CHAMP
OF ENGLAND

As he did push-ups in my small, London hotel room,
my old friend chanted the names of great boxers.

ALI. FRAISER. DEMPSEY. SUGAR RAY.

He wore Doc Martins, secondhand suit pants
and a black wool sweater.

He was sweating and panting
as I watched young, clean-cut English pop stars
dancing and lip-syncing on television.

When he finished his push-ups,
my old friend took a long drink
from the bottle of wine
he'd brought up from the hotel pub.

NO MORE DRUGS. He said.
NO MORE CIGARETTES AND NO MORE BOOZE.

He took another swig from the bottle.

THIS DOCTOR SAID I WAS GONNA DIE
UNLESS I CLEANED UP SO I'M GOING INTO TRAINING.
I FOUND THIS GYM AND I'M GONNA START
TOMORROW WORKING OUT, YOU KNOW,
AND MAYBE SPAR A FEW ROUNDS.

He wiped the sweat off his face
with the wine bottle as I lit a cigarette.

My old friend had moved overseas
a few years earlier and became a cult hero.

He once wore woman's make-up,
black leather pants, turquoise jewelry,
feathers in his dyed blonde hair
and black undertaker jackets.

He hid his southern California accent
by talking like a snake-handling Mississippi preacher
who'd lost faith in Christ and converted to voodoo.

The English ate it up.

He took another sip of wine
and started doing sit-ups.

FOREMAN. TYSON. LISTON. PATTERSON.

Before he moved to London,
he lived with his mother in a tract home
and his heroes were the usual suburban kid heroes;
dead or soon to be dead, misunderstood,
self-destructive rock stars.

DURAN. SPINKS. LOUIS. GRACIANO.

My old friend finished the sit-ups,
grabbed the wine bottle
and sat on the edge of my bed.

YOU SEE, WE WERE IN THIS PUB, he said.
A PUB WE ALWAYS HANG IN
AND WE WERE PRETTY FUCKED UP, YOU KNOW,
AND DRESSED LIKE WE USED TO DRESS,
he took a cigarette from my pack
and I lit it for him,
AND I'M WEARING THIS COWBOY HAT.
I GUESS IT WAS THE HAT THAT BUGGED
THESE SOCCER ASSHOLES IN THERE AND ONE OF 'EM
KNOCKS IT OFF MY HEAD AND STARTS CALLING ME
"YANK FAGGOT" AND SHIT LIKE THAT
AND CALLING MY WIFE A WHORE
AND NAMES I WON'T REPEAT.
WELL, THAT DID IT, I WAS SO PISSED
I THREW A PUNCH AT THE UGLIEST FUCKER
AND THEN ALL OF THEM JUMPED US
AND WE WOUND UP IN THE HOSPITAL.

He drank more wine.

I'M USED TO PEOPLE CALLING ME NAMES
BUT NOBODY, NOBODY, NOBODY
CAN SAY THINGS LIKE THAT TO HER.
NOBODY.

He drank the last of the wine.

I looked at my old friend,
sweating on my bed,
but all I could say was something weak like,
"That shit happens anywhere"
and "I'm sorry, man."

We didn't say anything for a while.

We watched the happy pop singers on tv.

I'M GONNA RUN DOWNSTAIRS FOR ANOTHER BOTTLE,
he said as he got up from the bed,
YOU WANT A BEER OR SOMETHING?

THE BARS OF LONG BEACH

The bars of Long Beach
are old and tired
but still put out when challenged
like an old journeyman boxer.

The bars of Long Beach
are strung out in long straight lines
of dusty neon from downtown
like the Christmas lights
behind the bar
that were put up in '61
and never taken down.

The bars of Long Beach
have bartenders that have heard
every story a hundred times
but would be happy to hear them again
while a jukebox plays
nothing newer than
1965.

The bars of Long Beach
are rough at the edges,
in need of paint
like the alcoholic ex-hooker
who never forgets a name
but can't remember
a face.

The bars of Long Beach
sit on quiet corners,
not bothering anyone,
like the guys inside
watching the football game
wondering why
it ain't them on TV,
it could have been them,
you know.

The bars of Long Beach
are full of old lovers
and drunken kisses,
drunken as the love song
being sung
by the guy passing out
in the bathroom.

You can get laid in them
but it won't mean anything
and some people like that
about the bars of Long Beach.

You can get as drunk
as you want,
pledge undying friendship
to the stranger next to you
as he talks about his truck
parked up on Signal Hill,
you don't care about his truck
or him
and he doesn't care about you

and some people like that
about the bars of Long Beach.

You can argue in them.
You can fight in them.
You can kill or be killed in them
but nobody would hold a grudge
as long as it makes
for a good story to tell
when you're drinking
in the bars of Long Beach.

EVENING BLUES

Standing at your open kitchen door,
smoking another cigarette,
watching you make a cup of coffee.

Your hair combed back,
still wet from a shower
and last night's make-up
washed off your face.

Both of us barefoot.

Both of us silent.

Both of us hungover
from the night before
and worn out from
talking and fighting
and talking and fighting
all day.

Last night everything was easy,
when we were drunk
and horny
and everything in the world made sense.

Tomorrow morning,
I have to go home
and I can't tell if you want me to stay

or leave
and, maybe, you can't tell either.

I watch a distant lightning storm
in the purple, evening sky
and listen to the soft rain
on the roof.

We glance at each other
across the kitchen,
say nothing
and then look away.

I think of an old blues song
and sing it to myself,

    I want to hold you, baby,
    but I don't know what to say
    I want to kiss you, baby,
    but I'm scared you'd push me away.

and I wish you could hear me

and I wish I could hear what blues
you sing to yourself.

PURGATORY

I was watching *Wheel Of Fortune*
when Janis called complaining
that there were no decent men
in Los Angeles.
Okay, I said.
She said they never called
her back after she slept with them.
You're very lucky, I said.

I'd fallen asleep on the couch
when Richard's call woke me up.
He said songwriters in this town
didn't hang out together anymore.
That's not altogether a bad thing,
I said.
Richard said if we stuck together
L.A. wouldn't be such a bad place to live,
it could be like Austin or Nashville,
where people care about songs
and songwriters.
I told him to call next week
and we'd get together
to eat or something.

Around 10:30, the bathroom faucet
came off in my hand.

After two in the morning,
while playing guitar

on the edge of my bed,
I heard gunfire
outside my bedroom window.

I laid on the floor for a minute
and then stared from the window
as six police cars
pulled in front of the house
across the street.

The next morning,
walking down the kitchen stairs,
I saw a parrot
fly out of the pine tree in my backyard.
I'd heard for years about parrots
that had somehow escaped their cages
and were living wild
in the hills of Silverlake and Echo Park,
but I'd never seen one before.

I watched the bird fly away,
its vivid green, red and yellow feathers
disappearing into the grey,
exhausted sky.

SAN FERNANDO VALLEY NO. 2

Marina has a bad hangover
but manages to fix coffee and eggs.
She doesn't remember what she drank
or if she took one drug or more.

Marina doesn't remember
the name of the guy in her bed
but she does remember
her audition at eleven o'clock
with a rock band in Hollywood.
Marina wants to be a singer.
She sips and stares
out her kitchen window
to the hamburger stand across the street.
The illegal aliens have lined up again,
waiting for someone to come by and pick them up
for one day of cheap labor.

THEY LOOK LIKE HOOKERS
ON SANTA MONICA BOULEVARD. She thinks.
A pickup truck
driven by a blonde man
in a T-shirt that says ROCK AND ROLL
pulls up to one group.
He waves for four and five get in.

The man from the bedroom
straggles into the kitchen naked.
WHY DO THEY BOTHER? Marina says.

WHO? He says.
THOSE MEXICANS, WHATEVER THEY ARE.
OH. He says.
Marina finishes her coffee
but she ignores her eggs.
The naked man eats them for her.
She goes back alone
to the bedroom,
does her make-up
and chooses what clothes to wear
for her audition.

JAYNE MANSFIELD

On the midnight, rural highway
(skidmarks on the pavement)
I thought of you, Jayne,
of your headless death,
your car ramming the back of a truck
in the Louisiana backroad night
countless news stories ago
and of how, before you died,
I slept with you in puberty,
your breasts
on crumpled Playboy pages,
hard nipples pressing
through a tight swimsuit
like maturity through
my skin.

GLAMOUR GIRL

She wore high heels in the daytime
when she'd stroll Hollywood boulevard.

She wore high heels shopping for groceries
at the Boys market on Highland.

She wore them when she hung out
at Raji's, the Zero-Zero or the Whiskey.

She wore them six hours a night
when she worked as a bartender.

She always wore them when we had sex
and her sharp heels would scar my legs.

She would take them off to sleep, though,
but when she'd get out of bed

in the middle of the night to use the bathroom,
she'd slip back into her high heels

just to walk the eight feet
from the bedroom to the bathroom,

and I'd lay in bed, listening to her high heels
clacking on the cold tile floor.

MADONNA'S KISS

The volume on the television is turned down
as I listen to a distant American voice
from armed services radio on a walkman.

The only thing on television is MTV
so I stare out the hotel window
at the snow-covered streets of Oslo, Norway,
as the American voice calmly describes
the first air attacks on Baghdad.

It's after two am and the bombing
has been going on for a couple of hours.

I look at the tv as Madonna french kisses a man
then she french kisses a woman.

The American voice sounds so far away,
far away as a Nebraska truck stop
or the bars on South Street in Philadelphia.

The American voice has none of the soul
of a Mississippi gospel singer
or the swagger of a drunk cowboy.

Madonna licks her lips
as a woman dressed in leather bondage gear
grabs a man's crotch.

I think about Lincoln and surf music.

I think about bar-b-que and Thomas Jefferson.

I think about my lover back in Los Angeles.

I think about the kids piloting the bomber jets
and how they've never known another president
besides Reagan.

I think of how they grew up watching MTV.

I think of how many would trade their bombs
for one night in the sack with Madonna.

I think of how many wouldn't.

I try to think of something that connects it all.

I try to think of something consoling.

I try to think,

as the bland American voice
fades in and out,

as the bombs fall,

as Madonna smiles.

BURLESQUE LIVES AGAIN

Robert and I sat in his car, drinking beer,
watching a small crowd of anti-pornography
demonstrators in front of the old
neighborhood movie theater.

The marquee said
    BURLESQUE LIVES AGAIN
    JEANIE NICHOLS
    WITH DAUGHTER ROSE
    TONIGHT ONLY

We waited until the beer
gave us enough guts to cross the picket line
and try to convince the old woman
in the ticket booth
that we were really sober eighteen-year-olds
who had somehow misplaced our I.D.s
and not drunken seventeen-year-olds
who couldn't get a date this Friday night
or any others.

Ten dollars each convinced her.

The theater had once been the showpiece
of post-war blue collar main street
but the factories of
South Gate, Paramount and North Long Beach
were laying off now instead of hiring

and the young white couples with money
preferred the new, treeless tract homes
of Orange County to the small, 1930s stucco bungalows
on the streets of dusty, dying oaks and palms.

On a makeshift stage,
in front of a torn screen
where Chuck Heston had once delivered
the Ten Commandments
to auto workers' families, a young man,
in a leisure suit, told bad, obscene jokes
to thirty people scattered in the dark theater.
Robert and I sat down
at the end of the strippers' runway
next to a mother and son.
They were both drunk.
The mother kept a tight grip with her large hand
on a bottle of Jack Daniels,
her other hand on her son's knee.
The son didn't laugh at the comedian.

No one laughed at the comedian.

THE AD SAYS YER MARILYN MONROE'S GODSON,
the drunken mother yelled,
YOU DON'T LOOK LIKE HER!

The comedian walked up the runway to her,
happy that anyone was paying attention.
MADAM, I DON'T HAVE TO LOOK LIKE HER
TO BE HER GODSON.

The mother screamed,
YOU DON'T LOOK LIKE HER!
I THINK YER FULL OF SHIT!

The comedian laughed a Hollywood laugh,
turned to no one in particular and said
I HEARD YOU NORTH LONG BEACH OKIES
WERE A TOUGH CROWD.

The mother jumped out of her seat.
I AIN'T NO OKIE, YOU FAG BASTARD!
I WAS BORN IN KANSAS IN 1924!
The son laughed,
grabbed the bottle from his mother
and took a long drink.

I SHOWED HIM,
the mother said sitting back down again.

The show's stars were Jeanie Nichols,
a stripper over fifty
and her daughter, Rose.
Rose was the first on stage
dressed in a metallic purple swimsuit
and purple high heels.
The Stones' BROWN SUGAR blared through blown speakers
as Rose danced up the runway.
She was no stripper.
Her bumps and grinds were the same acceptable
bumps and grinds of a homecoming queen
at the high school prom.
But when she took off her bikini top

and held her small breasts in front of the drunken son
the audience came to life.
He sipped from the bottle
while his mother pounded his knee with her fist.

BITE 'EM! BITE 'EM! THAT'S WHAT THEY'RE FOR!
she urged.

I tried to laugh but was too nervous.
They were nice breasts.
She was beautiful, I thought.
Rose looked over at me.
I smiled my best smile,
my adult smile.
Sure, baby, what a jerk that guy is, huh,
not like me, baby,
I'm used to all that shit, baby,
even though you can't strip, baby,
I'll take you in a minute.

Rose smiled back at me,
moved in front of me
and leaned her breasts into my face,
rubbing them just for me.

I was glad I wore my good shirt.
I was glad I washed my hair.
And, Dammit, Robert, you're giving me your car
and you're walking home because
I'm taking Rose up to her Hollywood apartment
for a long night of love.

YOU'RE CUTE.
Rose whispered as one of her hands moved slowly down
to her panties.
I wanted to scream.
I wanted to sweat.
I wanted to grab her breasts.
I wanted to kiss her purple lipstick lips.
But all I could do was stare.
I didn't want her to think I was like all the rest
of these North Long Beach Okies,
only concerned with her naked tits,
only concerned with her purple panties.
DAMMIT!
I'm different!
She must have seen or felt I was different.
This theater,
this dying city,
this youth and virginity
were only temporary.
Goddammit, someday I'll be drinking wine
in downtown Paris while this drunken mother's son
will be lucky if he gets a job
cleaning gas station toilets on Atlantic Boulevard!

Rose's hands went between her legs,
slowly up her thighs.
OH BABY, I LIKE YOU A LOT, she whispered.
She pulled her panties halfway off
and smiled at me with her tongue licking
those purple lips.
YOU DO THE REST, BABY.

The mother slapped my back.
HOLY JESUS, YOU GOTTA GIRLFRIEND, BOY!
Rose was really mine.
HELL, YES! PULL OFF HER UNDERWEAR!
Rose shoved her high heeled shoes
right into my stomach
and writhed in ecstasy on her back.
I could see the black hair between her legs.
I took a series of long deep breaths.
I got my courage up
but
the drunken mother leaned over
and ripped the panties off Rose's legs.

I GOT 'EM! I GOT 'EM!
She screamed.

Rose got up and danced back down the runway,
naked.
The song ended as the drunken mother
waved the panties above her head,
screaming victory.
Her son half-assed pleaded,
OK, MOM, YOU BETTER GIVE 'EM BACK.

Rose's mother Jeanie appeared naked
except for a silver G-string, silver cowboy hat
and silver cowboy boots,
dancing to RHINESTONE COWBOY,
shooting silver cap pistols
at the people along the runway.

Jeanie Nichols had the right bumps and grinds,
the kind of bumps and grinds you can only know
after thirty or forty years
in front of every drunken audience,
in every smoky joint
on every dying main street
in every forgotten city.
Men howled from the dark seats,
none louder than the mother, though.

NOW THAT'S A REAL STAR, she said.
GET A LOOK BOYS 'CUZ HER KIND
ARE GOING OUT LIKE THE DINOSAUR.

Rose stood on the dark side of the stage,
smoking a cigarette,
watching her mother.
As the theater light came on
Marilyn Monroe's godson thanked us for coming.

Robert went out to the car
but I waited for Rose to come out from backstage
and take me with her.
I waited until a security guard
told me the show was over
and
GET THE FUCK OUT OF THE THEATRE.

Outside, the demonstrators had gone home
and the marquee was blank.

I REALLY THOUGHT I HAD HER,
I said to Robert as I got in his car.
SHE JUST DOES THAT TO KEEP FROM GETTING
BORED,
he laughed.

We drove aimlessly around North Long Beach
until Robert suggested
that there still might be enough time
to pimp some more beer,
park across the street from our high school
and make fun of the people on dates.

And there was.

SAN JOAQUIN VALLEY NO. 1

A teenage girl
works the night shift
at a self-serve gas station
in Modesto.

She says little
but what she does say
is without a smile
and through a hole
in the window.

She wears
an orange and pink uniform
under the shadowless
yellow fluorescent lights.

All the customers
make jokes
as a cold wind blows
across the valley
but
she doesn't laugh.

NATIONAL CITY 1979

A hot afternoon

A bright purple diesel cab is parked
on hard, uneven clay
in front of a four room house

Blue house paint is chipping,
exposing large, irregular shapes
of grey plaster

Inside,
a woman is in bed
smoking cigarettes

(ashes fall on her white skin,
she brushes them to the linoleum floor)

and listening to a stack of old 45s
on a just as old phonograph

She hears Little Anthony

YOU DON'T REMEMBER ME
BUT I REMEMBER YOU

She glances, every now and then,
at the green curtains
faded from too much sun
and cigarette smoke

A man is in the bathroom,
asleep in the tub

He's been in there a long time,
ever since Don and Dewey sang

AND SO I'M LEAVING IT UP TO YOU
YOU DECIDE WHAT YOU'RE GONNA DO

The woman puts out her cigarette
in an overflowing ashtray,
plays with her ring unconsciously
and stares for a minute
at the white plasterboard ceiling
and the brown water stains in the corners

A new cigarette
as Don Julian and The Meadowlarks sing

HEAVEN AND PARADISE

The last record in the stack

She gets out bed,
turns the stack of records over
and listens to the B-sides play
as the sky slowly turns orange

A few miles away,
on the border,
men and women crawl under barbed wire,
follow a coyote,
look forward
then run

THE POWAMU KACHINA DANCES
ON THE HOPI RESERVATION,
ARIZONA 1993

We're not wanted here.

There are signs along the highway,
on the Hopi reservation,
advertising kachina dolls,
jewelry, rugs and pottery for sale
at various roadside curio shops.
These shops are not in the ancient
pueblos on the three mesas
but in the modern villages
on the desert floor.

The signs outside the pueblos say,
NO WHITES ALLOWED
or
NO NON-INDIANS ALLOWED
WITHOUT A HOPI GUIDE
or
NO OUTSIDE WHITE VISITORS ALLOWED
BECAUSE OF YOUR FAILURE TO OBEY
THE LAWS OF OUR TRIBE
AS WELL AS THE LAWS OF YOUR OWN.
THIS VILLAGE IS HEREBY CLOSED.

We're not wanted
and I wonder what I'm doing here.

The Hopis have lived on the three mesas
for maybe a millennium, maybe longer.
The Hopis were here before the Navajos,
before the Spanish, the Mexicans, the Americans,
the soldiers, the missionaries, the anthropologists,
the tourists, the hippies, the revolutionaries,
the Santa Fe turquoise trendies, the artifact collectors
and the artifact thieves.

The early settlers only wanted the Hopi's land
and the mineral wealth it contained
but now that we've got that,
we want souvenirs
or we want to show them not all whites are bad
or, maybe, we want the last thing they have left,
their religion.

The sacred kachinas were dancing
in the plazas of their pueblos
before Elvis, before Sinatra and Crosby,
before jazz, before television and movies,
before baseball and telephones,
before the Civil War and the Bill of Rights,
before the first slaves were brought to Virginia
and today,
the kachinas will be dancing again.

And I wonder what I'm doing here.

The first time I came to the Hopi mesas
was with my father and brother
during one my father's union organizing trips.

I was 5 or 6
and I remember my father,
standing on top of an old truck
in the plaza of one of the pueblos,
giving a speech to the Hopis,
some of whom worked
in the nearby copper and coal mines,
about the benefits of organized labor.

The next summer
we lived in Flagstaff for a month
and my father bought me my first kachina doll.

I made up a story
about having been a kachina in another life
and I pressured my parents
into driving me into the San Francisco mountains
outside of Flagstaff, because an old Hopi woman
had told me that was where the kachinas lived.
I stared out of the car window,
looking between the cottonwood and pine trees,
searching for any signs of kachinas.
"Any second now, we'll see 'em" I said.
They drove me until the road ended.
"They must not have recognized you." My father said.

I've collected kachina dolls ever since.

Thirty years later
I've returned to the Hopi mesas to finally see
the kachinas dance.

It's February,
the period in the Hopi ceremonial cycle of Powamu.
The Bean Dance.
Actually a series of dances
celebrating the miracle that,
in the dead of winter,
beans sprouts
are able to grow inside the village kivas.

We're not wanted
and I wonder what I'm doing here.

Outside the village of Hoteville,
on the third mesa,
there are no signs saying whites not allowed.
There are no signs for souvenirs
or for authentic Indian fry bread.

The winter afternoon is cold and clear
as I walk down the dirt road to the village plaza,
trying to rationalize being there.
I remind myself of my childhood fantasy
of being a kachina but that's not why I'm here.
I remind myself of sneaking into blues bars
with my brother when we were teenagers
to see Big Joe Turner and Lightnin' Hopkins.
I tell myself that I'm an American
and that in order to understand
what being an American means,
I have to understand and see America
and its history,
in all its greatness, brutality,
hypocrisy and secrecy.

The dreams we were taught in school
and the reality we live day to day.
I have to understand
our history that we invented
and built statues to
as well as our history we hide
in ghettos and barrios,
barrooms and graveyards,
skid rows and folk songs
and our history we hide
on Indian reservations.

I tell myself that I'm an American
and because I'm an American,
I have to see the kachinas dance,

just like I had to see Muddy Waters
or George Jones sing,

just like I hiked in the High Sierra
and through the Smithsonian,

just like I got drunk in Chicago,
Houston, Nashville and Seattle,

just like I stood on the battleground
at Gettysburg.

But as I stand in the adobe village,
surrounded by a few hundred Hopis,
watching the kachinas appear
out of the roofs of the kivas,
listening to their moans, grunts and singing,

(Their voices sounding similar
to old gospel/blues singers
like Blind Willie Johnson and Skip James),

listening to the rhythm
of the rattles in their hands
and the turtle shell gourds tied to their thighs
and the frightening swats of the kachina's yucca whips,
and their sacred, ancient songs
whose meaning I'll never know
in a language I'll never understand,
I feel like I'm not an American at all.

I feel more
like my immigrant Polish grandparents
must have felt
when they arrived
in this strange, new country,
looking at an America that didn't want them,
wondering,
just like me,
why they were here.

UTAH, AUTUMN 1983

There's a stiff dead cow
on the side of a two-lane highway
that heads west to Nevada
or east to the warm, morning sun
rising
on the Confusion Mountain range
covered with last night's fresh snow.

The stiff, dead cow
was shot in the stomach and head
on the highway side of the fence.

Last night
someone got drunk in Abraham
or Oasis or Hinkley or Delta
or Gunnison.
Last night someone got drunk
and got their rifle
and thought about shooting
his wife
or his kids
or himself
or a cow.

OLD WHITE WOMAN ON VERMONT 1982

It's no longer
Benson's Drugstore
but Botanica Alvarez
and the old white woman
on Vermont
walks
alone
through a crowd
of young Latinos.

She frowns at loud cumbias
blasting from car radios
and babies
crying from apartment windows,
her arms clutched
against
her breasts.

The old white woman
on Vermont,
wearing
a faded yellow day coat
and a dirty black hat,
rests at a bus stop
and stares at
her swollen feet,
her pink skin
sweating
in the brown heat.

SAN JOAQUIN VALLEY NO. 2

The valley is flooded
and the middle-aged farmer,
mud up to his knees,
digging long ditches
hoping the water will drain
from his field,
pays no attention
to his black and white dog,
barking as it jumps
at a traffic sign
again and again,
falling each time
back into one of the farmer's
new muddy ditches.

COMING HOME 1988

The night I came home to Los Angeles
I saw three teenage vatos
kicking a transvestite in front of a bar.

They tore at his skin-tight, white dress
as he tripped in his high heels
and fell on the sidewalk.

I circled around and pulled in front of them,
honking my horn like an idiot.
The vatos stared at me laughing.

The transvestite ran, screaming,
down Silverlake boulevard
and I quickly drove away.

She was in bed waiting for me,
with the sheets pulled down.
While I'd been gone she'd moved the bed
against the wall away from the window
with the bullet hole in it.
She was listening to her opera tapes
because we didn't have air conditioning
and she said the music made her feel
like she was in a climate controlled concert hall
and not in our hot apartment.
She said she was going stir-crazy
since our car had been stolen

while I was out of town.
She wondered if we couldn't
keep my rent-a-car for a few extra days
and drive up north where it might be cooler.
I told her I just got home
and didn't want to leave.

We tried to make love for the first time
since I'd left town a month before
but she stopped us, saying it was too hot.

The next morning, some guy down the block
shot up his apartment building.
When the cops came he shot at them
and they shot back.
His body was still in the street,
face down, as we drove past
on our way to breakfast.
She didn't say anything when I told her
I'd have to leave next week.

;ION

ARE YOU GOING OUT TONIGHT?
She asked.

It was one of those days,
during one of those weeks,
that she didn't get out of bed.

YEAH, I THOUGHT I MIGHT.
JAKE'S HAVING A JAM SESSION AT SOME BLUES BAR
AND HE ASKED ME TO SIT IN
AND I HAVEN'T PLAYED GUITAR IN A WHILE.

YOU'D GO WITHOUT ME?

I DIDN'T THINK YOU'D WANT TO GO.

ANY OF YOUR OLD GIRLFRIENDS
GOING TO BE THERE?

NO. IT AIN'T THAT KIND OF GIG.
JUST SOME LOUNGE GIG OUT IN REDONDO.

YOU'RE JUST GOING TO LEAVE ME HERE,
ALONE?

YOU HAVEN'T GOTTEN OUT OF BED
ALL DAY, I JUST KIND OF FIGURED . . .

YOU COULD HAVE ASKED.

WELL, DO YOU WANT TO GO?

NO. NOT NOW.

ARE YOU SURE?

YOU OBVIOUSLY DON'T WANT ME TO GO.

NO, IT WOULD BE FINE IF YOU CAME.

FINE? FINE? WELL, FUCK YOU,
YOU FUCKING ASSHOLE.

LOOK, WHAT IS YOUR FUCKING PROBLEM?

YOU'RE MY FUCKING PROBLEM,
YOU AND YOUR FUCKING OLD GIRLFRIENDS.

I'M NOT FUCKING MY OLD GIRLFRIENDS.

NO ONE WOULD.

FUCK YOU.

FUCK YOU.

When I walked out to my car
I could hear her screaming
at me from our apartment.

I sat in the car for a few minutes
not sure what to do,
still able to hear her screaming
even though the windows were rolled up.

YOU WEREN'T REALLY GOING TO LEAVE ME ALONE,
WERE YOU? She said, softly, as I came back inside.

I didn't say anything.

She held onto me and I held her,
her face pressed hard to my chest,
my shirt wet with her tears.

I KNOW YOU STILL LOVE ME.
I KNOW YOU DO. She said.

THE FIRST YEAR WE LIVED TOGETHER

The first year we lived together,
after she moved to Los Angeles,
she wouldn't get a job.

She said she couldn't get a job
because she didn't know how to drive
and, she said,
you'd have to be crazy to ride the bus
because if the criminals didn't kill you
the bus drivers would.

She'd stay in bed all day, reading,
or on the couch
watching television.

I CAN'T PAY FOR EVERYTHING. I'd say.

I'D GET A JOB, she'd say,
BUT THIS FUCKING CITY IS SO STUPID.
YOU CAN'T DO ANYTHING WITHOUT A CAR.

Eventually I found a car for her
and taught her to drive.

She got her first few jobs
as a receptionist
through a temp agency
until she found a full-time receptionist job

for some coke dealer
turned wanna-be movie producer
in Beverly Hills.

That job lasted a few months until
the coke dealer/movie producer took her
into his office and showed her his closet
full of latex and leather bondage gear.

He put his hands on her ass
and she quit.

IS EVERYONE IN THIS FUCKING CITY
FUCKING INSANE?
She asked me in bed later,
crying as I held her.

NOBODY IN THIS CITY HAS ANY FUCKING MANNERS.
YOU ASK A STRANGER A SIMPLE QUESTION LIKE
"HOW ARE YOU?" AND THEY'LL START TELLING YOU
ABOUT THE ABORTION THEY HAD TWO YEARS AGO
OR HOW MUCH MONEY THEY MADE LAST WEEK
OR HOW BIG THEIR FUCKING DICK IS.
CAN'T THEY JUST SAY "FINE. THANKS. AND YOU?"
I THINK IT'S BECAUSE EVERYBODY OUT HERE
THINKS THEY'RE SO FUCKING TALENTED
BUT, YOU KNOW WHAT, THERE'S NOT ONE
REAL PAINTER HERE AND THERE'S NO ONE
WHO CAN WRITE ANY DECENT POETRY
AND THE SUPPOSEDLY GREAT MUSIC SCENE
IS NO BETTER THAN DAYTON, OHIO'S
AND EVEN THE SYMPHONY ORCHESTRA SUCKS,

NOT THAT ANYONE IN THIS TOWN WOULD KNOW,
AND THERES NOT EVEN A COOL PLACE TO GO
TO JUST DANCE TO HALF DECENT MUSIC
WITHOUT SOME ASSHOLE GRABBING MY TITS
AND TELLING ME HE'S A PHOTOGRAPHER
FROM *PLAYBOY*,
LIKE THAT'S SUPPOSED TO FUCKING IMPRESS ME.
WHY DO I FUCKING STAY HERE?

After that,
she went back to spending her days in bed
or on the couch in front of the tv.

AFTER WE HAD SEX

After we had sex

After she left Virginia for Los Angeles

After she moved in with me

After we lived together for two years

After she asked everyday if I still loved her

After I told her I did

After her first serious anxiety attack

After she wouldn't get a job

After I quit two bands

After I went into debt to keep my own band on the road

After a three hundred pound guy wearing a purple negligee,
      jumped in my car, while I was waiting for her
      to come out of a store, and kidnapped me at gunpoint,
      saying, JUST DRIVE AND I WON'T KILL YOU

After I said PLEASE DON'T FUCKING KILL ME

After he threw the gun down when we saw a cop

After he and I fought for control of the wheel

After the cop arrested him

After I testified against the three hundred pound man
    and he was sentenced to prison for two years

After I went broke and sold off my rare guitars

After I broke up my band

After she had more serious anxiety attacks

After she started seeing a therapist

After we started fighting every day

After we lived in three apartments

After we spent four days not saying a word to each other

After we stopped having sex

After I cheated on her once

After we started seeing a couples counselor

After an old lover died of AIDS

After we took the AIDS test

After we tested negative

After I spent two months living in Nashville

After I was dropped from my record label

After I caught meningitis

After I spent two and a half weeks
    in two different hospitals

After I didn't get paid for a tour I only did for the money

After her car was stolen

After she worked a succession of receptionist jobs

After she asked everyday if I still loved her

After I lied to her everyday

After she found a decent job downtown

After guys at her job started asking her out

After we decided there was no reason to stay together

After we looked for three months at apartments for her

After she finally found one she liked

After I paid her first and last month's rent
    plus the security deposit

After I moved her things into her new apartment

After I waited for the gas person, the phone person,
     the cable tv person

After I told her to call me if she ever needed anything

After she asked me if I still loved her

After I lied one last time

After I left her alone in her new apartment

After I ate dinner alone that night at a Chinese restaurant

After I opened my fortune cookie

my fortune read,

ANY ROUGH TIMES ARE NOW BEHIND YOU.

A POEM FOR CHARLES BUKOWSKI

I once lived with a woman
      who owned doubles
      of every F. Scott Fitzgerald book

IF YOU REALLY LOVED ME, she'd say,
      YOU'D BURN YOUR BUKOWSKI BOOKS!

Already, in the name of love,
      I'd quit smoking in the bedroom,
      stopped talking to most of my close friends
      and thrown away a small collection
      of porno magazines
      and even an autographed copy
      of Bob Flanagan's S&M love sonnets

But the Bukowski books
      was where I drew the line

NO! I'd tell her
      and sometimes that ended the discussion
      and sometimes it didn't

When it didn't, she'd harangue me
      with all the criticisms
      usually thrown at Bukowski
      like a non-smoker preaching the evils
      of secondhand smoke

and I, like a smoker praising the joys
  of tobacco, tried to explain
  what it was like when I saw him
  read (my first poetry reading)
  in a small bar in Long Beach in the mid-'70s

I tried to explain what it was like
  seeing an old white guy as tough and cool
  as the old black bluesmen I'd grown up seeing

How the bar was so crowded
  that all I could see
  (above the drunks and hecklers,
  the English professors and the students
  and all the young men pretending
  they'd seen and done all that old men had)
  was his head

His face scarred and unshaven
  hair greasy and combed back,
  the kind of face you used to see
  on the old men in the old bars
  on the old streets like Western,
  Atlantic and Vermont

I tried to explain what it was like
  seeing a man who
  at a time when rock and roll meant nothing
  and everyone said HAVE A NICE DAY,
  understood the silent madness
  of an empty room

A man who understood men,
        men like my father,
        men who passed out drunk at kitchen tables
        or on bathroom floors,
        who spit out chunks of their lungs
        while fumbling for another cigarette,
        men who felt so much
        they prayed to feel nothing

But I tried hardest to explain to her
        how I left the bar that night
        with words pounding in my skull
        for the first time
        like a good rock and roll song

His words

Words like nothing I'd been taught in school
        but had felt every day of my life

And I tried to tell her
        how from then on I wanted to write
        (poems, songs, anything)
        and how, like the old bluesmen
        gave me music,
        Bukowski gave me words

I never burned my Bukowski books
        and I haven't seen the woman
        I lived with in years

I guess
        I really didn't love her

GENE VINCENT'S LAST SHOW

It was Oldies Night
at the Hollywood Palladium,
1970-something,
and the back-up band vamped
BE-BOP-A-LU-LA.
Art Laboe introduced Gene Vincent
and the crowd cheered
as Gene walked on the stage
limping on his lame leg.

I was fourteen
and that night had already seen
the standard L.A. oldies acts:
Bobby "Mr. Rockin' Robin" Day
Sandy "Teen Beat" Nelson
The Olympics singing "Western Movies"
Rosie breaking old hearts
with "Angel Baby"

and they were all fine.

But this was
GENE VINCENT!
This was special.

He was sweating in his leathers
under the hot lights,
mumbling his words,

trying to sing low, sexy and young.
Sing, Man.
Sing like he could still
put cigarettes out
on Johnny Burnette's arm.
Sing like he could
before booze and obscurity.
Sing like he could
before he held Eddie Cochran,
dead,
in his arms.

But he couldn't.

It wasn't there.
After a few bars he quit singing
but motioned for the band to continue.
A woman and three kids joined him
on stage.
She put her arm around Gene
and the kids stood around his lame leg.

I couldn't tell if he was crying
or if it was the hot light sweat
as he said:

I'VE HAD A LOT OF HARD TIMES
BUT THANKS TO THE LOVE OF MY FAMILY
MY HARD TIMES ARE IN THE PAST

The crowd cheered.

AND I'M READY TO ROCK AGAIN!

And the crowd screamed,

WELCOME BACK GENE!

as Gene and his family
left the stage.

Gene Vincent died a month later.

Years later,
Rockin' Ronnie Weiser told me
the woman and kids were fake.
Someone hired them for the night
because Gene's real wife had divorced him
and taken the kids
months before
his last show.

MEMPHIS, TENNESSEE, NOVEMBER 1981

There's forty people out there in the audience
in a club that holds three hundred.
I'm backstage in a cement dressing room
with a broken mirror
and a nude light bulb hanging from the ceiling,
drinking Budweiser and smoking Kools.

And there's forty people out in the audience
in a club that holds three hundred.
Ten of them are on the guest list.
We have to do three sets
and we're working for the door.
We're minutes from Graceland
where Elvis died.
We're minutes from Sun Studios
where this rock and roll stuff was born.

The club has posters of rock stars on the walls.
Rock stars playing big sports arenas
in front of thousands of fans.
Rock stars sweating out their cocaine and limousines.
And some guy asks if I'm gonna boogie tonight.
And the club owner says,
"I thought you guys were popular."
And the bar maid says,
"No more free beer."
And people are walking out before the first set.

LONG DISTANCE INFORMATION
GET ME THE FUCK OUT OF MEMPHIS TENNESSEE!

Back home people hate us that used to like us
and people hate us that always hated us,
the bank won't cash your press kit
and Nashville wants to cancel.

ELVIS IN THE ARMY

It was nighttime,
when Elvis was in the army,
I was three or four
and lost at a county fair.
I was inside a large, side-show tent,
getting knocked in different directions
by the legs of the crowd
and tripping myself onto the sawdust floor
when, through a break in the crowd,
I saw Shirley Temple singing
TOOT TOOT TOOTSIE GOODBYE
on a makeshift stage.
Seeing the little girl from tv movies
I forgot I was lost.
I stopped and watched.
When she finished
a man in a dark suit hustled her offstage.
He came back on stage smiling.

GUESS WHAT I GOT FOR YA!
I WENT AND GOT ELVIS BACK FOR YA!

Some girls screamed and some men booed.
One girl shoved me aside to get close,
then another.

I WENT OUT AND KIDNAPPED ELVIS
JUST SO HE COULD SING FOR YA TONIGHT!

More girls were screaming now
and more men booed.
I worked my way through the girls' skirts
and the men's legs to the side of the stage.
I knew who he was.
I'd heard Elvis on the radio
just like everybody else
and I liked him
just like everybody else
and just like everybody else I thought
he was mysterious,
as mysterious as the county fair
with the strange animals and frightening clowns.
I never doubted it was him.
I knew the man in the dark suit was bad
because my mother had already told me
about kidnapping.
The bad man scared me as he chanted,

I GOT HIM FOR YA!

making the girls scream louder
and the men boo louder.

I GOT HIM FOR YA!
I GOT HIM FOR YA!
I GOT HIM FOR YA!
I GOT HIM FOR YA!
I GOT HIM FOR YA!

The screams and boos reached their peak
as Elvis walked out on stage, a guitar over
his shoulders wearing his gold suit.

AIN'T YA GONNA THANK ME?
AIN'T YA GONNA THANK ME?
FOR BRINGING YA
ELVIS!

The girls around me were crying.
Elvis strummed his guitar.
As he began to sing,
the men booed but so did some of the girls.

IT'S NOT HIM! IT'S NOT HIM! cried one girl.

IT'S NOT BUT IT'S GOTTA BE! another said
running away from the stage.

Soon everyone was walking away.
Elvis was still singing
while the bad man in the dark suit
laughed at the disbelievers,

I TELL YA IT'S ELVIS.
I TELL YA IT'S ELVIS.

Elvis was still singing
when someone opened the tent flap
next to the stage.
I could see the ferris wheel outside.
Elvis was still singing
as I walked out of the tent
towards the bright carnival lights
in the dark nighttime sky.

SAN JOAQUIN VALLEY NO. 3

The man in the white uniform
picked up the blood stained
safety helmet
while some other men,
who had stopped to help,
pushed the bent frame
of the motorcycle
into the weeds along
the interstate.

The man whose truck
had blood on the fender
smoked a cigarette
while crouching next
to his large tires.

The birds, who had
built their nests under
the overpass
out of twigs and brown mud,
scattered from their homes
as the ambulance driver
turned on his siren.

THE MUSIC BUSINESS

I was seventeen when I played
my first paying gig in a bar.

It was a biker/drug dealer/ex-cop
hangout in an industrial zone
on the south side of Downey.

As I got out of my car,
carrying my flute and saxaphone cases,
I saw two bikers kicking some guy in front of the bar.
He was stretched out on the sidewalk
moaning.

His face was bloody and swollen.

ARE YOU IN THE BAND?
said one of the bikers
while still kicking the guy on the ground.

I said, YEAH, as nonchalantly as possible.

COOL, MAN. PLAY GOOD. he said.

I'LL TRY MY BEST. I answered,
quickly walking into the barroom.

BIG JOE TURNER

Every juke joint
boogie woogie pianist
three day rent party
4 am tenor saxophone battle
Kansas City black woman
California white woman
New Orleans Creole
every tapping foot
every dress slit up the side
every shot of whiskey, vodka and gin
every blues song
every song that ever swung
every Chicago ballad
and New York rhythm and blues shuffle
every Saturday night kiss
every Sunday night tear
everything that was good and right
everything that had love for the world
is in a grave in Gardena.

LIFE ON A RANCH

1

I'D LIKE TO LIVE ON A RANCH, she said.
We were in bed
drinking beer naked.
I GREW UP ON A RANCH. I HAD MY OWN HORSE
AND A COUPLE OF GOATS. WE HAD TO SLAUGHTER
THE GOATS AND THEN I HATED RANCH LIFE
BUT AFTER A WHILE I GOT OVER IT.
YOU GET USED TO IT,
IT'S JUST THE WAY THINGS ARE ON A RANCH.

I told her about my uncle.
He and his wife had a ranch
with horses and goats, and chickens,
the whole package.
My uncle loved his ranch
until his wife ran off
with one of the local cowboys.

I WOULDN'T LEAVE YOU, she said.

I JUST CAN'T SEE MYSELF ON A RANCH, I said.

YOU'D BE FINE AFTER YOU GOT USED
TO GETTING UP EARLY IN THE MORNING.

I WOULDN'T GET USED TO KILLING GOATS, I said.

I'D KILL ANY GOATS
THAT NEED KILLING, she said.

We drank some more beer,
smoked a cigarette
and made love for the third time
that morning.

2

We were sitting on the side of the bed.
She was crying.
I put my arms around her.

I'VE BEEN THINKING ABOUT THAT RANCH, I said
trying to cheer her up.
YOU REALLY NEED THOSE HORSES AND GOATS.
WE COULD HIRE SOMEONE TO DO THE WORK.
WE COULD SLEEP IN LATE,
GO RIDING IN THE AFTERNOON AND
HAVE THE GANG OUT TO DRINK ALL NIGHT,
BAR-B-QUES AND SHIT LIKE THAT.

She stared at me.

YOU KNOW RANDY, HE'S GOT A HORSE
AND HE DRINKS MORE THAN THE BOTH OF US
COMBINED,
I said.

She didn't smile but she had stopped crying.

WE COULD TAKE A DRIVE,
GO UP TO CENTRAL CALIFORNIA,
LOOK AT SOME PLACES, SEE WHAT THEY COST.
MAYBE RENT ONE OR SOMETHING.

YOU THINK SO, REALLY? She said closing her eyes.

I lit a cigarette.

SURE, WE'LL SPEND OUR EVENINGS ON THE PORCH,
DRINKING BEER AND LISTENING
TO MY RHYTHM AND BLUES RECORDS.
NOW THAT'S LIVING.
I said while accidentally blowing smoke in her face.

YOU WANT A BEER OR SOMETHING?

I got a beer from the kitchen, drank it
and imagined life on a ranch.
She had fallen asleep.
I woke her up.
Then we fucked.
Then I fell asleep.

3

YOU'RE DRUNK AGAIN, she said.
I REALLY HATE YOU WHEN YOU'RE DRUNK.

I was sitting on the floor.
The lights were out

and I was on the phone.

I'M SORRY, BABY. I KNOW IT'S LATE.
BUT I HAVEN'T TALKED TO YOU IN A WHILE.
I WAS THINKING ABOUT THE OLD RANCH.
YOU KNOW, I COULD BE PRETTY GOOD
AT KILLING THOSE FUCKING GOATS,
YOU KNOW.

THE ONLY THING YOU'LL EVER KILL IS YOU.

C'MON, THINK ABOUT THE HORSES.
THINK ABOUT THE COWS. WE COULD HAVE COWS.
WE COULD HAVE CHICKENS.

She didn't answer.
I sat on the floor
with the lights out
waiting.

She said nothing.

THINK OF THE OLD RANCH, I said.

She hung up.

MY MOTHER FELL

My mother fell this afternoon.
My mother fell
and hit her head on Grandmother's
jagged wooden table.
Strips of her flaky skin
clung to the table's sharp edge.
I let go of her.
I let go of her because
she said she was cold.
I left her standing alone
in her walker
as I went for her sweater.
But the drugs
or the chemotherapy
had taken away her coordination
and she lost her balance
in her walker
and she fell.
I let go of her.
My mother fell this afternoon
like she was a baby
taking her first steps.
The pink skin of her forehead
quickly turned purple.
A small slash of blood
dripped into her half-closed eyes.
My mother fell this afternoon
and my tears fell into her eyes
as I tried to lift her back up.

My mother fell this afternoon.
My tears with her blood.
My mother fell this afternoon.
My mother fell.

THE GREAT POET'S WIFE
(for Linda B.)

I understood why she was his muse
when one night, after a few beers,
I asked her
who her least favorite poet was.

She smiled like Dante's Beatrice
and said
WHY, ALL OF THEM, OF COURSE.

LEE ALLEN

The cigarettes that killed you,
you can smoke all of them you want,
now that you're in heaven.

Now that you're in heaven
each day will start in the late afternoon
with a casual round of golf

followed by a recording session
in the early evening and every heavenly session
pays triple scale and royalty points.

You'll have a gig every night,
now that you're in heaven, you and your sax
backed by a solid, bluesy organ trio

in an intimate, smoky niteclub
full of beautiful, smiling women
of every size, age, shape and color

and there'll be children sneaking inside
to learn the truths only you can teach them
about life and love and music

and when it's time for you to play in heaven,
you'll set down your scotch as a
sweet, black angel hands you your horn.

THREE SONGS

1

His hair was greased back
and he played old country songs
on a red Gibson guitar
through a beat-up Fender amp
in the middle of the last pinball arcade
left at the Pike in Long Beach.

It was a hot summer afternoon
and the country singer was already drunk.

There were only a few kids in the arcade
and none of them paid any attention to him
but I was fifteen and thought he was great.

The old amusement park
had seen better days,
better hot summer afternoons
when its promenade was full of families
and sailors with new tattoos
and strolling lovers sharing saltwater taffy.

The tattoo parlor was still open
but the roller coasters, the haunted house,
the fun house, the sugar candy and corn dog stands
were all closed and boarded up.

The country singer was amazed
that a kid my age requested Lefty Frizzell's
I LOVE YOU A THOUSAND WAYS
and when I dropped all my pinball quarters
into his empty tip jar
he offered me a sip of his whiskey
from a paper cup.

It tasted harsh but good.

2

The white nightclub manager
announced from the stage
that Johnny "Guitar" Watson missed the first show
because "the pigs"
busted Johnny on his way to the gig.

It was the early seventies
and most of the audience at the Ashgrove yelled
FUCK THE PIGS.

I was thirteen or fourteen
and sitting with my brother
in front of the stage.

I said FUCK THE PIGS too.

The Ashgrove was that kind of club.

Anti-Castro Cubans were always firebombing the place
for one reason or another
and the interior walls of the club
were covered with Maoist propaganda posters
of smiling, uniformed Chinese youth
holding hammers and sickles, waving red flags
and staring proudly into a communist horizon.

The Ashgrove was also the kind of club
that booked a young, sexy and electric
R+B guitarist and singer like Johnny Watson
with an ancient, blind, religious, acoustic,
gospel-blues guitarist and singer like Reverend Gary Davis.

Most of the audience couldn't see a connection
between the two men and talked loudly
through Reverend Gary Davis' second set.

Someone said he was in his eighties.

His fingers moved slow and arthritic
on the neck of his guitar,
showing none of the jaw-dropping dexterity
of his old 78s from the '20s
or the albums he made in the early '60s
after he was rediscovered by the folkies.

His voice was weak and hoarse
and he'd interrupt his religious songs to cough
or to softly ask the noisy audience
to PLEASE, LISTEN TO ME, CHILDREN.
WHAT I'M TELLING YOU
ABOUT GOD IS THE TRUTH.

I'VE BEEN WHERE YOU ARE
AND I KNOW WHAT YOU'RE FEELING,
PLEASE, NOW, CHILDREN, LISTEN TO ME.

The audience, in no mood
to hear about Jesus and heaven,
kept talking anyway.

Someone yelled,
SHUT UP OLD MAN!
and another said
I DIDN'T COME HERE TO GO TO CHURCH.

But then, on his final song,
I WILL DO MY LAST SINGING IN THIS LAND SOMEDAY,
the powerful voice and guitar playing
of his old records returned
as if he'd been pacing himself all night
just for this song.

Incredibly, most of the audience shut up
as he sang the slow ballad,
his ragged voice booming through the club.

I WILL DO MY LAST SINGING IN THIS LAND SOMEDAY,
I DON'T KNOW WHERE I SHALL BE
JUST AS LONG AS MY GOOD LORD
STILL BELIEVES IN ME.

I lit one of the cigarettes
from the pack I'd stolen from my father
and tried to look cool even though
I was crying.

PLEASE CHILDREN,
he said when the song was finished,
PLEASE REMEMBER ME.
PLEASE REMEMBER WHAT I TOLD YOU.

Then he slowly rose from his chair
and walked off the stage.

A couple of months later he died.

In the meantime,
someone had bailed Johnny "Guitar" Watson
out of jail and when he finally played
he was as angry, loud and great
as he should have been.

3

He was bald
and only had three or four teeth left
but the old man smiled when he saw us
sit down at a table in the coffee shop
with an acoustic guitar.

It was long after 2am
and my brother Phil and his two friends,
Gary Masi and Dave Carroll,
had let me tag along earlier that night
when they snuck into Vina's blues club
down on Adams for the Sunday night jam session.

My brother was eighteen
and I was sixteen but Vina,
an elderly white woman,
didn't ask for our i.d.
and none of the black, middle-aged musicians
or the black, middle-aged clientele seemed to care
as we watched the jam session
and drank cans of Budweiser.

Later, in the coffee shop,
the old, bald, white man stared at us
but said nothing as Dave, Gary and my brother
passed the guitar back and forth,
singing songs for the waitresses,
trying to charm them for free food.

Besides the old man, we were the only customers
so the waitresses gathered around our table,
laughing and requesting everything
from Elvis to James Brown.

Eventually, the old man got up
from his seat at the counter
and slowly approached us.

He told us that he'd made a couple of records
when he was younger
but nothing ever came of them
and then he asked if he could, please, play a song.

The old man took the guitar gently into his hands.

It was obvious by the tentative way he held it,
slowly running his left hand
up and down the neck of the guitar,
that it had been a long time
since he'd played one.

At first he tried to sing an Ernest Tubb song
but as soon as he reached the first chorus
he coughed and phlegm dripped from his lips.

He stopped singing
and wiped the phlegm on his shirt sleeve.

PLEASE, LET ME TRY AGAIN. he said.
LET ME TRY THIS ONE I WROTE.
I WROTE IT FOR MY WIFE,
OF COURSE, THAT WAS A WHILE BACK.
SHE'S BEEN IN THAT HOSPITAL
JUST DOWN THE STREET
FOR OVER THREE MONTHS NOW.
SHE ALWAYS LIKED ME TO SING IT TO HER.

No one said anything
as the old man began a slow, country ballad.

His fingers had trouble making the chord changes
and he sang so softly,
as if he didn't care if we heard him or not,
that I couldn't make out the lyrics
but none of that mattered
because we could see the tears in his eyes.

We applauded when he finished
and one of the waitresses said his meal was on her.

THANK YOU. GOD BLESS YOU.
He said handing back the guitar.
I WISH YOU BOYS ALL THE LUCK IN THE WORLD
WITH YOUR GUITAR PLAYING.
IT NEVER GOT ME ANYWHERE
BUT I ENJOYED IT JUST THE SAME.
He wiped his tears
on the same sleeve he had wiped his phlegm.

The old man smiled,
showing his few remaining yellow teeth,
as he waved goodbye
and walked out of the coffee shop
down a dark and empty Imperial Highway
towards the hospital.

THREE OLD MEN

We ate a late breakfast in Mojave.

I was driving the three old men;
Jack, Tex and my father,
to a pack station north of Bishop
from where they'd go on horseback
into the Sierra for a month.

Over breakfast,
and for most of the drive up Highway 395,
the three old men discussed which politicians
were tolerable and which were opportunistic liars
or they complimented me on my Dodge van
but mainly they talked of their past Sierra trips
and how this one would be their best.

Now that the kids were grown up
and on their own,
it would just be the three old men
for a month of fishing
and nothing else.

Neither Jack or Tex
brought up my mother's death
the year before
and neither Jack or my father
mentioned the passing of Tex's wife
a few years earlier.

After checking into a motel for the night in Bishop,
we ate an early dinner and stopped at a liquor store
for two six packs of beer.

We sat around the table in the motel room
I shared with my father, drinking the beer.

The old men talked more about their trip,
more about how wonderful and relaxing it would be,
more about what supplies they were bringing,
more about what lakes they would fish,
about what bait and lures they'd use,
about whether the recent rains had ruined the fishing
and about how this really would be
their best Sierra trip ever.

It had been a long time since I'd been with them.

I hadn't seen Tex in over ten years
and hadn't seen Jack and his wife Louise,
since I'd moved away from home years before.

Their voices were softer
than I remembered from my youth
and they spoke to me as if I was almost one of them.

THAT'S A NICE VAN YOU GOT. A DODGE, HUH?
SEEMS LIKE DODGE IS MAKING THE GOOD ONES.
Tex said.

HOW LONG DO YOU THINK
YOU CAN MAKE A LIVING PLAYING MUSIC?

Jack asked.
SOONER OR LATER IT ALL ENDS, DOESN'T IT?
IT ENDS FOR EVERYBODY.
NOT SINATRA OR CROSBY, OF COURSE,
BUT JUST ABOUT EVERYONE ELSE.

I NEVER REALLY LIKED SINATRA,
my father said,
EVEN WHEN HE WAS A DEMOCRAT,
AND CROSBY REMINDS ME OF RUSS COLOMBO.
YOU REMEMBER RUSS COLOMBO?
SHOT HIMSELF IN '32 OR '31, I DON'T REMEMBER.

YOU HAVE SOMETHING TO FALL BACK ON,
DON'T YOU? A SKILL OR SOMETHING?
Tex asked,
lighting the one cigarette a day he allowed himself.

YOU KNOW, Jack said,
BACK WHEN I WORKED FOR THE SHERIFF'S
DEPARTMENT, I USED TO HEAR THAT RUSS COLOMBO
WAS MURDERED.
IT WAS ALL COVERED IT UP, THOUGH.

WELL, NOBODY GIVES A SHIT ABOUT HIM NOW.
My father said.

THAT'S THE IMPORTANT THING TO REMEMBER
ABOUT THE MUSIC BUSINESS,
YOU GOTTA SAVE YOUR MONEY
'CAUSE SOMEDAY NOBODY IS GOING TO CARE
ABOUT YOU ANYMORE. Jack said.

WELL, Tex said,
scratching his forehead
with the stub of his missing thumb,
YOU'RE STILL YOUNG
AND WHO KNOWS WHAT'LL HAPPEN TO YOU,
BUT AT LEAST YOU GOT A GOOD VAN OUT OF IT.
THAT'S MORE THAN MOST GET.

When most of the beer was gone,
Jack and Tex went to their rooms
and my father and I watched television.

WHEN ARE YOU GONNA QUIT? he asked me
as I lit another cigarette.
I SMOKED ALMOST THIRTY YEARS
UNTIL I QUIT. IT WASN'T THAT HARD FOR ME,
WHEN I REALIZED THOSE BASTARDS
ARE MAKING MILLIONS KILLING PEOPLE.

I told him I'd think about it.

YEAH, ONE DAY I JUST QUIT. My father said
as I dropped the cigarette
into a half-empty beer.

We left the motel at five-thirty the next morning
and were at the pack station in less than an hour.

As we unloaded their gear from the van
the three old men teased me about not going with them.

The breath of the horses and mules
steamed in the cold morning air

as they were saddled
and then loaded with the old men's supplies.

My father thanked me for driving them
and each of the old men shook my hand.

IT'S NOT TOO LATE TO COME ALONG. Tex said.

HE'S STILL TOO YOUNG. Jack said.
THIS TRIP IS JUST FOR OLD MEN.

WE'LL SEE YOU IN A MONTH. My father said.

I felt good driving back to Los Angeles.

The Owens Valley
and the northern Mojave desert
still looked the same
as it had twenty years earlier.

395 was still mainly a two lane highway.

Bishop, Independence and Lone Pine
were still small towns
without endless housing tracts
and mini-malls on every corner.

I felt that some of California still existed
the way I remembered it.

The old men were back in the Sierra.

There was still some continuity in life.

When I got home there was a message
from Louise on my answering machine.

She said she'd be at my house
by eight the next morning and she was.

As we drove up 395,
Louise tried about to talk
about anything other
than why we were driving back
to the pack station.

Louise told me how much she loved opera
and how much she hated the pope.

She told me about Jack's childhood in the Sierra
and how she and Jack met and fell in love
and how they'd known my parents since the late forties
and how much they loved them
and how much she missed my mother.

But I kept asking her the same questions.

Did the heart attack kill him?

She didn't know.

Was he already dead when he fell off the horse?

She didn't know.

Or did he die when his head hit the rocks?

IT WAS SOMETHING,
WATCHING THE HELICOPTER LANDING.
My father said
after we'd been driving a half-hour or so
in silence from the pack station.
THAT PASS IS PRETTY STEEP, YOU KNOW,
NOTHING BUT SLATE ROCK UP THERE
AND NO REAL FLAT PLACE TO LAND.
THE PILOT REALLY KNEW WHAT HE WAS DOING.

He stared straight ahead
as the afternoon sun,
setting behind the Sierra's eastern slope,
cast purple shadows
across the Owens Valley.

THAT'S THE QUICKEST WAY YOU COULD'VE
GOTTEN THE BODY OUT
Jack said a few minutes later.

Louise sat next to him in the back seat of the van,
one hand gently caressing his head
the other resting on his folded hands in his lap.

WELL, SURE. My father added.
IT WOULD TAKE A FULL DAY
TO BRING A BODY DOWN ON HORSEBACK.

POOR OLD TEX. Louise said.

Whenever the road was clear,
I'd glance over at the two old men
sitting quietly,
but neither of them looked back at me.

Their eyes focused
only on the highway
or the desert
or the jagged peaks of the Sierra.

Both of them had been to war
and both had killed.

Both had seen family members and friends die.

Jack had spent his adult life drawing murder scenes,
murder victims and murder suspects
for the sheriff's department.

My father was at the liberation
of the concentration camp at Dachau
and had to photograph its victims and survivors.

Respecting their knowledge of death,
I didn't bother them with questions.

But as I drove south on 395,
I started thinking
that, maybe,
their silence wasn't just a way of coping,

that, maybe,
despite all the death they'd seen,
they still didn't know what to say about it,
they still didn't know what words
could make any sense of it
or what words could offer
even a hint of understanding
or maybe there really is nothing to say about it.

HE WAS PROBABLY DEAD
BEFORE HE HIT THE GROUND.
My father finally said.
after a couple of hours.

PROBABLY. Jack said,

YEAH, HE PROBABLY NEVER KNEW WHAT HIT HIM.
My father said
as the evening lights of Mojave and Lancaster
slowly spread across the desert floor.

After we dropped off Jack and Louise
and unloaded the camping gear,
I sat with my father in his kitchen.

WHEN ARE YOU GONNA QUIT? He asked
as I lit another cigarette.

THE FIRST TIME HE HEARD
HANK WILLIAMS

He remembers a light bulb
hanging
above a stable door
on a warm evening.
Moths, June bugs, mosquitoes
circled the bulb
or rested on the peeling paint
of the wooden door
in the bulb's yellow glow.

The windows of his mother's
dark, green Studebaker
were rolled down.
He remembers it was quiet
except for the sound of crickets
and his mother nervously
jiggling her car keys
and her breath
exhaling cigarette smoke.

They were waiting for his aunt
who had gone into the stable
with a man wearing a cowboy hat.

His family had spent the day
at his aunt and uncle's ranch
in the foothills at the edge

of Los Angeles' 1950s sprawl.
He can't remember why
his aunt had to leave the ranch
or why his mother had to drive her
to another ranch
or why he had to go with them
or why his aunt went into the stable
with the man wearing a cowboy hat.

He can't remember if his uncle
said anything to his aunt as she left
or if he kissed her goodbye
or if his uncle stood on the porch
watching the car lights disappear
into the black canyon.

He remembers the man in the cowboy hat
coming out of the shadows of the stable.
He remembers his aunt getting out of the car,
following the man back inside,
the stable door closing behind them.

He remembers standing up on the car seat
and staring at the closed stable door.

He remembers a song
coming from someplace.
It played once and then again.
HEY GOOD LOOKIN'
was all he remembered from the song.

When he was older,
smoking his first cigarettes
and drinking his first beers,
he heard the song again
and remembered
curling up on the front seat,
resting his head on his mother's lap
and falling asleep
as his mother hummed the melody
long after the record
had stopped playing.

TALKING TO PLANTS

An ancient Filipino man lives next door.

I see him every morning from my window

standing in his front yard.

He's always barefoot and wearing the same clothes;

a purple sweater, khaki pants and an old straw hat.

His front yard is full of ferns.

Every morning, as he waters his ferns,

he talks to them.

COCKSUCKERS. MOTHERFUCKING COCKSUCKERS.

He says.

His ferns are healthy, full and dark green.

Sometimes, very early in the morning,

he screams at his ferns.

FUCK YOU, YOU GOD DAMMED, SON OF A BITCH
COCKSUCKERS!

He'll do this until the Mexican guy across the street

threatens to kill him.

The old Filipino will call him a cocksucker.

The Mexican will call him a puta.

This happens every week.

Once a woman with a baby visited him.

HELLO COCKSUCKER. He said to the woman

as she handed him the baby.

He held the baby at arm's length and smiled.

HELLO LITTLE MOTHERFUCKER.
DON'T TAKE NO SHIT FROM NO COCKSUCKERS,
MOTHERFUCKER.

Once, while I was working outside on my balcony,

I hit my thumb with a hammer and yelled FUCK.

The old man, standing in his garden, yelled back,

SOUNDS LIKE SOMEONE SUCKING COCK!

One day, two young white guys,

smiling and wearing suits and ties,

were canvassing the neighborhood.

They were Jehovah's Witnesses.

The old Filipino was sitting on his porch,

leaning back in a wooden chair, legs crossed,

his hat pulled down over his eyes

like a confident sheriff in an old western.

GOOD MORNING, SIR.
MAY WE SPEAK TO YOU FOR A FEW MINUTES?

The Jehovah's Witnesses said,

walking into the old man's garden,

not waiting for him to answer.

The old man rose quickly from his chair

and, shaking his fists, ran towards them, yelling,

ME, ME, ME JOHN WAYNE, YOU COCKSUCKERS!
ME U.S. FUCKING MARINES, FROM THE HALLS
OF MONTEZUMA TO THE SHORES OF TRIPOLI!
YOU GOD DAMMED, SON OF A BITCH
MOTHERFUCKERS.

The missionaries weren't smiling

as they quickly left his garden.

After the intruders had gone,

the old man walked among his ferns,

singing an old Bing Crosby song,

MOONLIGHT BECOMES YOU.

When he finished singing,

he sweetly told his ferns,

THAT SONG WAS FROM 1942,
YOU COCKSUCKERS.

A PRAYER FOR LOS ANGELES 1979 - 1986

Our Lady, Queen of the Angels, Queen of the Chumash and Gabrielino Indians, Queen of Gaspar de Portola, Pio Pico, Kit Carson, pueblo of sweating desert winds, oasis of burning canyons, downtown looming above unmarked founders' graves — mezitos, indians, blacks — who trudged from Mexico to Mission San Gabriel then down Mission boulevard to settle on chaparral river flats. Their ghosts haunt pawnshop storefronts, tits and ass theatre lobbies on Bella Union Main street. Skid row, no longer home for road weary Woody Guthrie or road jazzed Kerouac slumming 1940s burlesque houses, just men sleeping in plastic trash bags and cardboard boxes in front of the midnight mission or men with throats slashed beneath artists lofts or throwing up on the steps of city hall. Queen of the women silently waiting for buses in front of Mexican bars, Cuban bars, Guatemalan bars, Vietnamese bars, Chinese bars and old white men bars where the old white men play big band on the jukebox so they won't hear the Spanish outside in the dying palm tree streets of Phillip Marlowe stucco and heat apartments. Our Lady of limousines, of Hollywood movie and tv stars, dead stars, rock stars, has-beens, hopefuls, directors, producers, their scripts, their lunches, their homes, their tennis courts, their motorcycles, their bodyguards, their Mercedes washed and their lawns mowed by illegals who wait for crumbs on street corners. Our Lady of Musso and Frank's and Graumann's Chinese where Bible belt tourists try to fill the shoes of John Wayne and Shirley Temple. Virgin Mother of Santa Monica Boulevard street corner boys staring numb at passing cars, of heartbroken queens boasting dried blood wrists and negative test results. Hookers, pimps, tricks and some guy working all night behind the counter of an adult book store, someone working all night behind bulletproof glass at a self-service gas station, someone working all night selling lottery tickets at a convenience store, religious cult apostles handing out throw-a-way pamphlets of throw-a-way salvation and heavy metal white boys cruising endless, identical suburban streets tempting the wilder side of blonde girls with eternal tans. Our Lady of KRLA lowriders cruising Whittier Boulevard past the Silver Dollar Cafe, past Ruben Salizar's ghost while east side vatos spray paint boundaries on hopeless walls. Queen of a south-central thirteen-year-old armed with an automatic weapon and a desperate heart that can't forget a past that still exists. Our Lady of drive-by shootings, of nervous police trigger fingers and choke holds. Our Lady, Queen of the victims of fires, landslides, earthquakes, of dark freeways. Queen of Native Americans, Hispanics, Asians, Whites from Pacoima to Little Tokyo to Little Seoul, from Torrance to Bell Gardens, from Fairfax to Boyle Heights, trying to get by just one more day underneath the air-conditioned views from the half-empty skyscrapers downtown. The unemployed aerospace workers and steel-workers of glamourless Maywood, Commerce and Gardena. The corporate computer drones of Westwood and Century City. The World War veterans who came here for the good life of sunshine in La Mirada and La Puente next to post card orange groves under snow-capped mountains but found themselves in imitation Spanish colonial tract homes, New England tract homes, imitation French provincial tract homes, imitation Bauhaus tract homes under exhaust brown skies the same as Chicago or Detroit. Our Lady of cars. Our

Lady of mini-malls. Our Lady of vanished Chumash and Gabrielinos, of vanished hillsides, vanished ranchos, vanished citrus groves, vanished Angel's Flight, vanished Pan Pacific, vanished red cars, vanished Garden of Allah, vanished Bunker Hill, of your vanished river. Our Lady of the Pacific Ocean, that brought Cabrillo and the Yankee whalers, that comes to the sand directed by you, through moon and stars, again and again, forever and ever, Amen.

EXCERPT FROM A DETECTIVE NOVEL I'LL NEVER WRITE

He'd had enough.

He'd seen enough dead bodies,
heard enough conflicting stories,
heard and told enough lies, smiled enough bullshit smiles
at people he'd rather kill.
He'd had enough of using his fists
or his gun on people who if someone had only loved
them enough sometime in their past maybe he
wouldn't have to kill them now.

He'd had enough of thinking.
He used to pride himself on his brain power.
Proud of his ability to see every angle to every story,
to see what everyone said was a lie was actually true.
His clinical ability to ponder
an unsolved mathematical problem
or picture the serene wilderness of Santa Cruz Island
while examining one more bullet hole
in one more dead man's face.

He'd stopped caring what guys were the good guys
and what guys were the bad guys.
He'd stopped caring who killed anyone anymore.
No one else cared anymore, why should he?
All he cared about was finding a new apartment,
preferably at the beach on the westside.

A new apartment in a new building
where everything worked.
A new apartment with security guards, private parking,
air conditioning, cable television, a swimming pool,
a jacuzzi and absolutely no ghosts
of ex-lovers haunting in his bedroom,
reminding him of promises made and broken
and promises never made but broken anyway.

And a new car.
A man his age deserved a good new car.
He didn't deserve to be stuck
in a San Bernadino Freeway traffic jam
on a ninety degree afternoon
with his heater on full-blast to keep
his '75 Chevy Impala from overheating.

Every night, after drinking his usual
half a bottle of NyQuil, he would lay in bed
imagining the joys of waking up brainless.
He'd pray to the god he no longer believed in
to please, please, please God,
somehow let him wake up satisfied with the world.
Satisfied with whatever the newscasters, newspapers,
Time Magazine, People Magazine, Entertainment Tonight,
corporate PR commercials, police spokespersons,
politicians, next door neighbors, auto mechanics, murderers,
lovers and television and radio talk show hosts told him.
One hundred percent satisfied with whatever toothpaste,
shaving cream, lite beer, gasoline, potato chips,
chewing gum, peanut butter, aspirin, hemorrhoid cream,
telephone system and underwear he bought.

He would love the music he hated.
He would sing along with any song
that came on the radio and buy any CD in the top ten.
He would go to see any movie that came out
and he'd love them all.
He would leave a movie theatre happy that such talented,
beautiful, selfless people made
such wonderful, entertaining movies.
He would wear the clothes everyone else wore
and he'd be happy.
Wear his hair like everyone else did
and he'd be happy.
Eat whatever food everyone else did
and he'd be happy.
He'd be so damn happy to give his money, happily,
to the people and products that made him happy.

Falling asleep, he'd fantasize about every dead body
he'd ever seen but instead of dead they were alive again.
Their wounds healed, they were gathered around the pool
of his new apartment, having a bar-b-que, telling jokes,
laughing, smoking and drinking beers with girls in bikinis
and calling him to come down and join in all the fun.
And join in all the fun.

Join in all the fun.

SPIDERMAN VERSUS THE KACHINAS

The Hopis in Shungopovi have closed their annual
Powamu kachina dances to whites this year.
Armed tribal police block the dirt road to the pueblo
with their jeeps to enforce the ban.

Several different Hopis told Nicole and I
that last year Marvel Comics put out a comic book
depicting kachinas
(The Hopis sacred supernatural and ancestral spirits)
as evil monsters.
The bad guys for some white super hero to fight
in order to save the world.

Outside a small adobe house in the pueblo of Walpi,
a homemade sign hanging in the window advertised
kachina dolls for sale.
Inside a young Hopi boy was drawing
and coloring in a notebook at a wooden table.
He wore a L.A. Raiders t-shirt
and was listening to a tape of Hopi vocal music.
Without smiling, he showed us two small kachina dolls
and when we said we weren't interested in buying them,
he shrugged and went back to his notebook.

Nicole and I couldn't help but notice that he was drawing
Marvel Comic's superhero, Spiderman.

IS SPIDERMAN YOUR HERO? Nicole asked him.

YES, HE IS. The Hopi boy said, still not smiling.

AFTER AN EARLY SNOWFALL
ON THE IOWA/NEBRASKA BORDER

The whole family was laughing
as they killed the rattlesnake.

The snake was crossing
an icy, two-lane highway
and maybe the family
in the minivan didn't see it
and maybe they did see it
but either way they drove on,
laughing.

ARE YOU GOING TO TELL HER?
I asked my friend.

We were standing by the side of the road
watching the rattlesnake's blood
steaming as it slowly spread
across the frozen pavement.

I'VE NEVER TOLD HER BEFORE
he said.
BUT SHE ALWAYS FINDS OUT,
SOONER OR LATER,
WITHOUT ME HAVING TO TELL HER.

He didn't smoke
but he bummed a cigarette off me.

The rattlesnake still tried
to get across the highway
even though its guts
were starting to ooze
out of the long gash the minivan's tires
had cut in its body.

I CAN'T HELP MYSELF SOMETIMES
he said.
I GUESS I STILL NEED TO KNOW
I CAN BE WILD, YOU KNOW?

I told him I knew.

The rattlesnake squirmed
in its blood and guts
as we smoked.

I GUESS,
I said,
THAT SNAKE DIDN'T KNOW
WHAT HIT IT.

I HOPE NOT,
my friend said
as we watched
the snake slowly die.

DRIVING INTO LOS ANGELES 1994
For Chris Gaffney and Greg Leisz

1

The sprawl has reached the desert.

Driving into Los Angeles
from a four-month tour,
I see they've built a post-modern,
retail outlet mall in the Mojave
between Barstow and Victorville.

Housing tracts and condos
are leapfrogging the San Gabriel Mountains,
turning the desert into suburbia

and making me feel so fucking old.

Everything changes in southern California
and changes so quickly that
landmarks and landscapes disappear
in a year, a month, a week, even in a day,

and I often find myself
sounding like a old man:

I REMEMBER WHEN THIS WAS A DESERT.
I REMEMBER HILLS COVERED WITH OAK TREES.
I REMEMBER SMALL TOWNS SURROUNDED

BY ORANGE AND AVOCADO GROVES.
I REMEMBER THE SWEET, ORANGE PERFUME
FROM THE GROVES IN THE MORNING AIR.
I REMEMBER AFTERNOONS
WHEN THE WIND BLEW IN FROM THE OCEAN,
ACROSS THE DAIRY FARMS
OF ARTESIA AND BELLFLOWER,
HOW EVERYTHING SMELLED LIKE COWSHIT.
I REMEMBER FORESTS OF EUCALYPTUS TREES
AND BAMBOO JUNGLES FULL OF SNAKES,
JACKRABBITS, LIZARDS, AND HORNED TOADS
ALONG THE CONCRETE BANKS
OF THE SAN GABRIEL RIVER.

But everything changes in southern California.

Everything has to change.

Everyone has to live someplace.

Everyone has to work someplace,

grow up someplace,

move away from someplace,

eat someplace,

sleep someplace,

die someplace.

And so the sprawl reaches
from Ventura to San Clemente,
from Lancaster to Long Beach
and it's reaching for Bakersfield and Indio,
reaching further and further
from the collapsing downtown core
like the flaring nova of a dying star.

And, sometimes,
I feel so fucking old.

2

The air is brown and thick
as I drive out of the El Cajon Pass,
through the outskirts of San Bernadino,
and I'm thinking of how many times,
for how many years,
from how many tours,
I've driven home on this interstate
and how many times,
for how many tours,
I've driven away.

I'm thinking of how many musicians,
roadies and friends have driven this road,
back and forth, with me
in beat-up, borrowed or rented vans,
never quite making it big enough for a tour bus.

I'm thinking of how many of them
have nothing to say to me anymore,
after sharing their worst jokes and deepest secrets,
their broken hearts and dreams of success
on endless drives from one bar gig to another,
and I,
having shared the same,
have nothing to say to them.

I'm thinking how many have given up this dream
and quit the road.

I'm thinking how many have disappeared
and how many have died.

Passing Pomona,
I turn on KRLA,
all oldies all the time.

Gladys Knight sings,
WITH EVERY BEAT OF MY HEART,
and I'm thinking of the lover
who waited for me
the first time I ever drove away
on this interstate
and how long she waited
and I'm wondering who
she waits for now.

As the Chi-Lites sing OH GIRL,
I'm thinking of the other lovers
who've waited for me.

The lovers
who laid down with me
in the dark dirt between rows of orange trees
or beneath the pines in the San Gabriels
or between cold motel room sheets
and I'm remembering
what sweet lies and truths
we whispered and believed
and I'm wondering
who they believe now.

I'm thinking of the lover
who's waiting for me now,
while the Penguins sing EARTH ANGEL,
and how she says
she'd do anything
to keep me from leaving again
and I'm wondering how much longer
she'll say that.

The afternoon traffic
on the San Bernadino freeway is jammed
as Curtis Mayfield and The Impressions
sing KEEP ON PUSHING.

I'm remembering seeing Curtis Mayfield
perform at the Palomino
in front of less than a hundred people,
just a few weeks before the accident
that left him paralyzed for life.

A year or so before I saw him,
I'd quit writing songs,

bitter, angry and fed up
with trying to survive as a musician.

That night Curtis sang
KEEP ON PUSHING and PEOPLE GET READY,
like it was still the sixties,
like an audience of thousands
were hanging on every word,
like the songs still meant the same to him
as they had when he wrote them.

My friend, Rosemarie, kept screaming,

THERE'S NO JUSTICE IN THIS WORLD!
SO AND SO IS A FUCKING MILLIONAIRE
AND CURTIS IS PLAYING THE PALOMINO
AND THE FUCKING PLACE IS EMPTY.

and she may be right,
that there's no justice in the world,
but I left the show that night
believing in Curtis,
believing again in the power of his songs,
believing in the power of all great songs.

Believing songs
can still get you out of bed in the morning
when you feel no reason to do so.

Believing songs
can still heal loneliness and a broken heart.

Believing songs
can still teach us to not kill each other,
even if it's only for three minutes.

Believing songs
are still worth all the frustrations
and disappointments
and joys
of a life playing bars along the interstate.

Believing, again,
that songs are still worth living for.

Landscapes are raped
or disappear,
music scenes and styles
and family
and friends
and lovers
come and go

but you keep on pushing.

As corny as it sounds,
Curtis is right,
you keep on pushing.

You keep on pushing.

You keep on pushing.

Songwriter, guitarist and singer Dave Alvin grew up in Downey, California when there were still orange groves. Alvin studied writing at Long Beach State University with Richard Lee, Elliot Fried and Gerald Locklin and studied music in barrooms. In 1979, with his brother, Phil, he founded the legendary roots-rock band, The Blasters. Alvin later was a member of the influential punk band X. Since 1987, he has concentrated on his own solo albums, *Romeo's Escape* (Razor and Tie Records), *Blue Boulevard, Museum of Heart* and his latest *King of California* (all on Hightone Records), as well as producing other artists. He has also worked on the soundtracks of several high and low budget films such as John Waters' *Cry Baby* and Allison Anders' *Border Radio*. His songs have been recorded by many artists including Dwight Yoakam, Joe Ely, Buckwheat Zydeco, Marshall Crenshaw and The Paladins. He currently divides his time between his home in the Silverlake section of Los Angeles and the national interstate highway system. He also smokes too much.